LIVING UNDER THE VOLCANO

Valentina Ga

Living Under the Volcano

CHRISTINE HAILES PERILLO
WITH VIVIEN CULVER

KINGSWAY PUBLICATIONS
EASTBOURNE

Biblical quotations are taken from
the New King James Version © 1979, 1980, 1982
Thomas Nelson Inc, Publishers; and from the
New International Version © 1973, 1978, 1984
by the International Bible Society

ISBN 0 85476 695 2

Co-published in South Africa with
SCB Publishers
Cornelis Struik House, 80 McKenzie Street
Cape Town 8001, South Africa.
Reg no 04/02203/06

Designed and produced by Bookprint Creative Services
P.O. Box 827, BN21 3YJ, England for
KINGSWAY PUBLICATIONS LTD
Lottbridge Drove, Eastbourne, East Sussex BN23 6NT.
Printed in Great Britain.

Contents

Acknowledgements

The work of the Philippine Outreach Centre depends first and foremost on the Lord, without whom I can do nothing, and then on all the people who faithfully help in so many ways. Of these, special thanks are due to the trustees who work for the Philippine Outreach from the UK; to my parents and Nanna Jean, for their wisdom and understanding and the many sacrifices they have made; and chiefly to my husband and children, whose support and patience mean so much when, as often happens, our work causes us to spend a lot of time apart.

Of those who have helped in the making of this book, thanks are especially due to Kevin Nicholas, for many hours spent helping to arrange the material; to Rita Fenwick, for the speed and efficiency with which she typed the manuscript; and to Fiona Gray, for drawing the map.

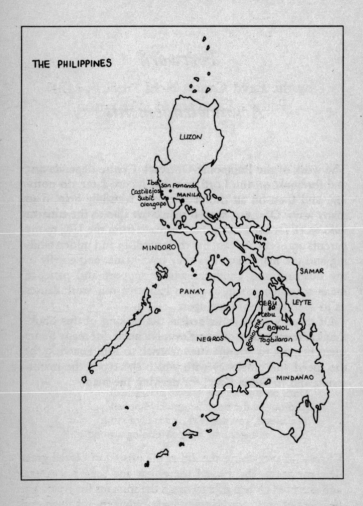

THE PHILIPPINES

LUZON

Iba San Fernando
Castillejos
Subic MANILA
Olangapo

MINDORO

SAMAR

PANAY LEYTE

CEBU
cebu
BOHOL
BOHOL STA. Tagbilaran
NEGROS

MINDANAO

Foreword

by the Revd Canon Noel Proctor, MBE
Former Chaplain of HM Prison,
Strangeways, Manchester

After arriving to take the post of Prison Chaplain at Strangeways, Manchester in 1979, I was introduced to a music group of young people from the Altrincham area. They were a talented group, but one young lady reminded me of the following poem:

> Two frogs fell into a deep cream bowl,
> The one was wise and a cheery soul.
> The other one took a gloomy view
> And bade his friend a sad adieu.
> Said the other frog with a merry grin:
> 'I can't get out, but I won't give in;
> I'll swim around 'til my strength is spent,
> Then I will die the more content.'
> But as he swam, though, ever it seemed
> His struggling began to churn the cream
> Until on top of pure butter he stopped,
> And out of the bowl he quickly hopped.
> The moral, you ask? Oh, it's easily found:
> If you can't get out, keep swimming around . . .

Chrissy, in everything she did at the prison, displayed great determination. She played the guitar and sang her songs, and she used all her gifts to reach the inmates for Jesus. Yet her gifts of music and singing were only a means to an end to get the ears of the men. This was followed by her directness with the gospel, which seemed somehow unexpected from such a slight figure of a girl.

She clearly knew that God's Holy Spirit was using her to win men for Jesus, so she was invited to come to the prison on a regular basis to share in groups and services. Early on she spoke of her firm conviction that her ministry would involve prison work, but as I pointed out to her, she was very young; she was also attractive and perhaps her naive and trusting nature could be easy prey for the 'con men'. Furthermore, I knew that in the British prison chaplaincy at that time, there was no possibility of her coming into a full-time ministry.

We talked about this, but she did not seem discouraged. And as we prayed for each other, the Lord began to show me that Chrissy had more than enthusiasm, a nice voice and an attractive personality. She had that wonderful gift of 'stickability', and I concluded that wherever the Lord would finally lead her, she was determined to trust him until the doors would open.

The remarkable quality which stands out in Chrissy's character and personality is her deep love for the Lord Jesus Christ, and her almost hungry desire to introduce others to him. This commitment has given her the determination and resolve to press on against seemingly insurmountable difficulties, and to prove her Lord in every situation.

The following story is so remarkable that it reads like a novel, and I know you will be blessed by it. It is also a real challenge to young Christians, to seek God's will for their lives, and to launch out into the deep waters for the 'catch' which only God gives.

1

'You Shall Receive Power'

'Every one of you will be baptised in the Spirit tonight.'

This statement by our visiting preacher at church that
evening was made with a confidence that astounded me.
'All of us?' I thought. 'Surely that can't be true.'

The speaker was Lewis Cardno, a retired fisherman from
Peterhead who travelled all over Britain singing and
preaching Christ. He had impressed me as being the
most joyful person I had ever met – not with a superficial
joy, but one that was deep and genuine. He'd been speaking about the power of the Holy Spirit, emphasising how
vital it was for all Christians to receive this power in order
to live lives that were truly pleasing to God. When he'd
finished, he had asked all those who had not yet been
baptised in the Spirit to raise their hands. Several of us
had done so and it was to us that he addressed those words
which so amazed me: '*All* of you. . . .'

My surprise was not due to any doubt about baptism in
the Spirit; my father (who was the pastor of the church),
my mother and many of my fellow church members had
already had this experience. It was due rather to the fact
that I was only thirteen. I had mistakenly gained the
impression that some Christian experiences were only for
adults because my parents had not yet allowed me to be

11

baptised in water as a believer, even though I'd been a Christian since the age of seven. Mum and Dad never tried to force the pace of my development as a Christian; they saw it as their task to teach me the way I should go and to leave the rest to God. When they said I was too young to understand the purpose of baptism in water, they, of course, were concerned only about my ability to grasp its significance, but I imagined that what mattered was my actual age. If I was too young to be baptised in water, how could I be baptised in the Spirit?

Now suddenly, Lewis' words took hold of me. I became certain I was included and I was filled with a sense of excitement and expectancy. There was no doubt in my mind that I would receive the Spirit that night. And I did. All of us who raised our hands were baptised in the Holy Spirit and began to speak with other tongues.

Would this be a passing sensation born of emotional excitement, or a life-changing experience that would radically transform my relationship with God and enable me to translate my faith into action with a new power? Time would tell.

From early childhood I had seen in my mother's life what it meant to put Christian faith into practice. Mum became a Christian at a Billy Graham crusade in Manchester in 1961, the year before I was born. Her own mother ('Nanna Jean') became a Christian at the same time.

Nanna Jean worked as a cook in a probation hostel for boys and would often talk over with Mum the sad stories these boys had to tell. She felt their troubles deeply and did everything she could to show them the love of Jesus. She would bake them special treats and spent hours listening to their problems and telling them about the love Jesus had for them in spite of the things they had done. Mum became as concerned as Nanna and because it was always impossible for her to keep God's love to herself, she had to do something practical for these boys who seemed to have been abandoned by society.

One of them, Derek, didn't want to go home when his time at the hostel came to an end. He was afraid that he would soon slip back into crime if he returned to his old haunts. And so, when I was just three years old, my parents invited him to come and live with us in our small three-bedroomed house. Mum's aim was to show Derek the love of Christ so that he might accept Christ for himself. It was different for Dad, though. He wasn't yet a Christian and didn't relish the thought of rebels like Derek invading the privacy of his home. However, he did want to please Mum and he knew she felt that this was something God was calling her to do.

In order to make room for this new member of our family, I had to squeeze into the smallest bedroom with my two brothers, Stephen, who was nine and Paul, five. This was fun for a while, but it didn't take long for war to break out. And the changes weren't over yet.

One afternoon, Nanna Jean was having one of her talks with Mum about the problems of the boys at the hostel. 'You see, Mary, once they get out they have nowhere to go. No one wants to help boys like them. What they really need is a home or some sort of centre. But who would do it?'

Dad looked at them over his newspaper and said, 'If you're so concerned, why don't you do it?'

Even though Dad wasn't a Christian, God used him to plant the seed of a vision in Mum's heart. She knew God was challenging her to provide a home not only for Derek but for other young lads in need. It was obvious that our house just wasn't big enough, so straight away Mum began to look for somewhere more suitable. She had no success for a while, and once again it was Dad who eventually pointed out the right direction. Looking through the newspaper one evening, he called out to Mum, 'Here's the house you need – 52 Barrington Road.'

This was a large house which had been a doctor's surgery; it had sixteen rooms, including nine bedrooms. Dad wasn't really serious. He showed Mum the picture and promptly forgot about it. But the next day, at his office, he received a phone call.

'Les, it's me. I'm in it.'

'What are you in, Mary?'

'The house.'

'What house?'

'52 Barrington Road.'

Such a large house wasn't at all Dad's idea of a family home, but he wasn't too worried because there seemed little chance of ever having to move there. Not only was it well beyond their price range but there was also a prospective buyer, a doctor. Mum wasn't at all daunted by this and confidently told the estate agent that God wanted her to have the house. Within a week she was proved right. The doctor changed his mind, and Mum and Dad were able to buy the house for £3,500 instead of the original price of £6,250. Dad had no option but to surrender and admit that God really did seem to be on Mum's side.

So in 1966 we moved the four miles from our small house in Sale to Barrington Road in Altrincham, leaving behind our unremarkable, average way of life for one that could hardly have been more different. In the years that followed, our extended family included many young lads who came to us homeless, jobless and with a history of being in trouble with the police. Sometimes whole families came if they were going through a difficult patch, and stayed until they were on their feet again. One of our most memorable guests was a tramp called Paddy, who was literally white with lice when Mum took him in and cleaned him up. She carefully warned me to keep out of his way, in case I caught lice too. Paddy, however, took a shine to me and often asked me to sit on his lap, and despite Mum's cautions I never had the heart to refuse, though I was always scared to death as I sat there.

A year or so after we moved, Mum invited Brian Smithyman to take a meeting in our home. Brian was an evangelist from a Pentecostal church in Wolverhampton, who had felt God call him to hold meetings in the Altrincham area. That meeting was the first of many and it was through Brian's ministry that Mum received the baptism in the Holy Spirit early in 1969.

It was now, too, that God began to work in Dad's heart, and shortly afterwards, alone in his bedroom, he had a life-changing experience. On the same night he was born again, baptised in the Spirit and healed of a painful injury to his spine, the result of a fall a year earlier. He was completely transformed. Instead of being glued to the television, he became totally absorbed in his Bible. Whereas before he had found satisfaction in a successful business career, he was now hungry for the word of God. He spent every spare moment in reading and studying. He didn't realise at first that in this way God was preparing him for a ministry of his own.

But within weeks, God had spoken separately to both Mum and Dad, directing them to go and see a Christian couple whom they hardly knew. Through this couple, God showed Mum and Dad that they were to begin to form a church at 52 Barrington Road, with Dad as pastor. So one of the bedrooms was cleared out and before long the Upper Room Christian Fellowship came into being. We had all kinds of people attending – families and quiet elderly folk mixed happily with former drug addicts and ex-prisoners.

And then there was the Sunday school, which was Mum's special work. Every Sunday afternoon, the peace and tranquillity would be shattered when a hundred or more children came bursting through the doors – and in a sixteen-roomed house, that's a lot of doors. Dad would go off to his study while Mum, in her element, spent the afternoon telling the children about the love of Jesus.

This was no ordinary, run-of-the-mill Sunday school. Along with the youngsters from Christian homes there were the ones whom Mum, quite literally, fetched in off the streets. She would drive a minibus through the roughest areas inviting them to join, and they came in large numbers – some from broken homes, some whose fathers were in prison, others whose parents were alcoholics. But to Mum, whatever their background, they were all just children who needed to know they were loved by the same Lord Jesus Christ.

Of course, I joined them in Sunday school, and when I was seven I gave my heart to the Lord. I had the advantage of a Christian home, I was brought up on the teaching of God's word and from early childhood I had seen faith in action all around me; so though I was very young, I understood that I was a sinner and needed a Saviour, and I believed that Jesus had died for me to save me from my sin and its consequences. I really did love the Lord, and I knew that I should show this by the way I behaved. But as time passed, I had to admit to myself that I was failing to live a life that was pleasing to God. The problem was that I had entangled myself in a situation where my love for God was in conflict with my need to gain acceptance and admiration from my school friends.

When our home was first opened to the lads from the hostel, I was a very cute three-year-old, and for several years I was a great favourite with them. Later, as I grew bigger and fatter, they noticed me less and less and I felt lonely and ignored. I often wished I had a sister, but since I hadn't I decided that if I didn't want to be lonely I had to become one of the lads. I thought that if I shared their interests and their habits they would notice me again, and so, unknowingly, I embarked on a course which led me into a lot of confusion and unhappiness.

It was one thing to compete with the boys on equal terms at football, but unfortunately I didn't stop there. I carried my search for a new identity into school, where I became very unruly and was often involved in fights with other children. I found I could hold my own against anybody – in fact I thought it was beneath me to fight with girls and only fought boys. I took pride in the fact that while my opponents were often reduced to tears, I never allowed myself to cry, however badly I was hurt.

In my heart I was ashamed of my behaviour and took care to hide it from my parents and church friends. I still loved attending church meetings and even sang an occasional solo, but all the time I knew my life was at odds with what I believed. By the time I was twelve I was living what was virtually a double life, and though I didn't want to be a hypocrite I felt powerless to change the pattern in which I was trapped.

When I moved on to secondary school, it wasn't long before many of my teachers had given up on me, I was so badly behaved. None of their punishments had any effect and within a year they had more or less written me off as hopeless. Because my life was such a mess, I never spoke to my classmates about the Lord; I wasn't ashamed of him, but I was ashamed of myself. I knew that people would expect much better of me if I professed Christ and I was afraid I would never be able to live up to their expectations. All my school friends lived a long way from my home and didn't even know I went to church, much less that I was a pastor's daughter.

I was desperately unhappy about my inability to be a good witness for the Lord. Despite my behaviour, I did love him and longed to be faithful to him. I couldn't do it in my own strength, but thankfully God's faithfulness to us always far exceeds ours to him and he granted me the desire of my heart that night when I was baptised in the Spirit.

I began now to experience in my own life the fulfilment of Jesus' promise. 'But you shall receive power when the Holy Spirit has come upon you; and you shall be witnesses to Me . . .' (Acts 1:8). I found I had a new boldness in telling people about the Lord Jesus and what he had done for me, and I was no longer worried about living up to their expectations because I had the power of the Holy Spirit to help me.

My school friends were not slow to notice the change in me. One day soon after Lewis' visit, one of the boys at school pushed me over, knocking me to the floor. Anticipating my usual reaction, he instinctively dived out of my way and was dumbfounded when I just picked myself up and didn't respond to his challenge. I hadn't even had to struggle to overcome the impulse to retaliate – it simply wasn't in my nature any more.

My attitude in class changed out of all recognition. My domestic science teacher, for example, who had been the target of some of my worst and most unco-operative behaviour, could hardly believe it when I voluntarily rewrote my notes for the whole year, so that they would be neat and tidy. Even more amazed was my PE teacher. Having struggled for so long to get me to move so much as a muscle, she now saw me becoming one of the most active in the class, running the cross-country course and eventually winning a place in several school sports teams. The joy of my new relationship with the Lord spilled over into everything I did, so much so that my English teacher took me aside and warned me that if I wanted to pass my 'O' level, I had to stop writing about my religious beliefs in every essay. But when he told me to write about my experiences, what else did I have to write about? Jesus was my life. I continued to write about the Lord, even in the exam (which I passed).

I worked hard at everything. Teachers were no longer my enemies but my friends and my mission field. I would never miss an opportunity to speak about the Lord. I would invite them to meetings and one or two even came along.

The baptism in the Holy Spirit was the beginning of a new and wonderful relationship with Jesus. I really wanted him to reign in my life and I was hungry to know more of the things of the Spirit. My father often entertained visiting preachers, with whom he would have long discussions and debates concerning doctrine, and I used to sit and listen whenever I could, silently soaking it all up. My father is a man of great spiritual insight and I loved to hear him speak of the deeper things of God. I never realised at the time how much the Lord was teaching me through these conversations.

God also had things to teach me directly. I wanted him to reign in my life, I wanted to do with joy anything he asked of me. In the summer of 1976, when I was fourteen, I learned a small but significant lesson about the meaning of obedience. Mum and Dad had taken me to a Christian camp run by the Hollybush Christian Fellowship in North Yorkshire. During one of the evening meetings, I became aware that the Lord had something particular to say to me that night. As I waited for him to make his will known to me, I had a strong sense of his presence, which continued long after the meeting was over. While other people were leaving, my parents stayed behind with me in the marquee, but didn't attempt to intervene as they realised that the Lord was dealing with me. At last, at around midnight, when the marquee was almost empty, he spoke to me: 'Christine, I want you to burn your records.'

Mum and Dad had bought me a record player the previous Christmas and I'd started to build up a collection of pop records which I'd hoped would one day match my brother's collection. I hadn't seen anything wrong in this before, but there and then I made up my mind that I would burn them and that I would not allow anything to alter my decision. It was a small sacrifice, I thought, and I didn't intend to exaggerate it; but obedience even in small things is important, and this seemed to be the least I could offer to the One who had done everything for me. I've since been asked how I knew it was the Lord speaking, but to me it was a simple matter: '. . . the sheep follow him, for they know his voice . . . they do not know the voice of strangers' (Jn 10:4–5). I knew his voice as surely as I knew my parents'.

The return to normal life after the excitement of a camp or convention is always an anticlimax. Away from the atmosphere of faith and expectation in the company of other Christians, I knew it would be easy to let my determination fade – I had seen this happen to other people. When we arrived home from Hollybush, I was already missing the fellowship we had shared with our friends there, and I certainly didn't have the same feelings as I'd had on the night when the Lord spoke to me. However, my father had taught me to live the Christian life by faith, not feelings, so I went straight to my room, gathered up my small collection of records and headed for the back yard. On the way, I met several of the young people from church, who wanted to know what I was doing. When I explained, they tried to persuade me that I should give the records to them. 'You'll still be getting rid of them,' they said. 'That's just the same as burning them.'

I felt terrible. I couldn't do what they asked, but I didn't want them to think I wasn't prepared to let anyone else have the records just because I couldn't keep them myself. But it wouldn't be the same; God hadn't told me to get rid of them but quite definitely to burn them. So I went ahead and did it. My parents didn't interfere, not even to praise me for being obedient. I have always been grateful for the fact that they never encouraged spiritual pride in me, and taught me instead that to be obedient to the Lord – to be a living sacrifice to him – was just my reasonable service.

Giving up my records was a small sacrifice, yet after I had done it I began to appreciate that by asking it of me the Lord had saved me from much that would have been harmful. Soon after, a school friend invited me to a party at her house. In the past, I'd accepted her invitations without a thought, but this time I had to refuse. 'God spoke to me and told me to burn my records,' I explained, 'so I'm sure he doesn't want me to dance to someone else's.' To my surprise, she respected my position and even continued to invite me to her parties, though she knew I wouldn't accept. I was grateful for her kindness, because no teenager likes to be the only one without an invitation, which became mostly true for me once my views became known.

Even though I never went to parties, I couldn't help hearing them talked about at school. Gradually, I found out what I had been too naive to realise before – that while I'd been enjoying the dancing in one room, other things were happening elsewhere. I learned that girls as young as thirteen and fourteen were getting drunk and losing their virginity as a consequence. I was so thankful to the Lord for saving me from that, and I realised that his salvation extended not only to forgiving the sins I had committed but also to keeping me from situations which could lead me into sin.

I once debated this subject with my eldest brother. Before giving his life to the Lord at the age of twenty-one, he had had some experience of the world and the sort of pleasures which it offers. He reasoned that the testimony of a person who had been rescued from the grip of such pleasures was more dynamic than that of someone who had never known them. I understood his point of view because testimonies of that kind do have a dramatic appeal. However, I knew that the only difference between a drug addict who had been saved by grace and someone like me was that whereas God's grace had set the addict free from addiction, that same grace had saved me from ever being ensnared in it. Either way, it was all due to grace.

Grace – and, by the power of the Holy Spirit, a new freedom to do what was right. I had so much to be thankful for. And so much still to learn.

2

'The Day of Small Things'

Nick was the leader of our church youth group, as well as of our singing group, which we called Psalm One-Fifty. More than this, he was also a gifted and dedicated evangelist, wholly committed to taking the gospel to the people of Altrincham. Every Thursday, whatever the weather, he would go out onto the streets with his Bible, a bag of tracts and his guitar. Occasionally, other members of the church would go with him, but not all of them had the same enthusiasm as Nick when it came to standing in the pouring rain, and some of them had other responsibilities which had to come first; so Nick often went out alone. But this never discouraged him. Week by week, with or without helpers, he went cheerfully on with his work. I really admired his faithfulness.

Then my admiration turned to conviction. Why was I just feeling sorry for him when I could go with him myself? Hadn't I been learning that the Christian life meant obedience and sacrifice? Well, here was another area where God was calling me to obey. The prospect filled me with fear, because my only previous experience of open-air evangelism had been as a member of a large group. It would be very different with just the two of us, but I knew I couldn't let my fear get in the way of my obedience, so I told Nick that I wanted to join him.

Every week, before we set out, Nanna Jean would pray for us and Nick would ask the Lord to direct us as to where we should go that day. It might be the bus station, the railway station, a pub or the middle of a crowded shopping centre. Nick had no fear of anything or anyone. By preaching and through songs given to him by the inspiration of the Holy Spirit, he boldly declared the good news of salvation through Jesus Christ.

At the beginning, I just tagged along in Nick's shadow, but gradually the Lord used him to train me in evangelism. Soon, as well as sharing in the singing, I was able to take my first steps in speaking to the passers-by. Though I was quaking inside, I learned to trust the Holy Spirit who was always faithful to give me the words I needed and bring to my mind the Scripture references which were appropriate in each situation.

Of course, as I'd foreseen, there were difficulties and discomforts to face. Sometimes it was rain or freezing cold; sometimes our pride was wounded when people laughed at us. But these were only physical and temporal discomforts. Through them all, we had the assurance of God's word that those who sow to the Spirit (Gal 6:8) will have a harvest that is not temporal but eternal. By helping Nick I was discovering that if in spite of our fears we step out and rely on God, he will use us however inadequate we feel. This truth was brought home to me even more by an experience which followed from my frustrating struggle to learn to play the guitar.

My interest in playing began when Mum and Dad bought a guitar as a Christmas present for my brother Paul. I was constantly borrowing it even though I knew it annoyed him – I so much wanted to learn to play. I asked Nick to help me, but somehow I didn't make much progress. All my attempts to discipline my fumbling fingers ended in failure. So I made a covenant with the Lord, that if he would help me I would play only for him and for his glory. I wasn't conscious of the Lord speaking to me about this, but he was very gracious and granted me my request, and before long I could play enough for a solo accompaniment. For my part, I resolved to play only for him.

By this time Dad had been involved in introducing the Full Gospel Business Men's Fellowship International (FGBMFI) into Britain, and was President of the Altrincham branch. Psalm One-Fifty, of which I was a member, were often asked to lead the worship at FGBMFI meetings, which might be either evangelistic events or opportunities for Christian men to have fellowship with each other.

On one occasion, when I was fifteen, there was a large FGBMFI convention in Blackpool. One of the items on the programme was the women's luncheon meeting, at which the speaker was to be Jean Darnall. As many of the men too were keen to hear her, Milicent Spilman, who was responsible for the meeting, had invited them to join us. This would make it a very big gathering – over a thousand were expected to be there. At the beginning of the conference, Milicent approached me with a request that almost stopped my breath: 'Will you minister in song at the luncheon meeting?'

My heart thumped and my mouth dropped open. I knew that I'd promised the Lord I would sing for him whenever the opportunity arose, but surely she couldn't mean me? Not on my own, in front of all those people? Milicent could see how nervous I was, but she didn't offer me an escape route. Instead, she encouraged me: 'You can do it; the Lord will anoint you.' Scared and reluctant, I agreed.

As the conference got under way, I became more and more afraid. Others who were to play and sing arrived with all their expensive equipment and backing tapes. They sounded so professional. I began to tremble at the thought of standing in front of so many people, just me and my acoustic guitar. But I couldn't back out; I knew, despite my inadequacy, that this was something God was asking of me.

I went to the Lord in prayer. I didn't ask him to give me a sweet voice or to help me avoid mistakes. As Milicent's words had indicated, it wasn't technical skill that I needed, but his anointing.

When the time came for me to sing and I heard my name announced from the platform, my whole body began to shake. Making my way unsteadily to the front, I encouraged myself with the promise of Philippians 4:13: 'I can do all things through Christ who strengthens me.' But the real battle hadn't started yet. As I began to sing, a voice whispered in my ear: 'You see, all that worry was for nothing. Look, they really like you.' I looked and, true enough, people did seem to be enjoying the song. 'You see,' the voice went on, 'you do sing well.' Then I knew that this was not the Lord's voice – he wouldn't use flattering words or encourage pride – but Satan's. Internally, I rebuked him. 'You were never anything but a liar. Without Jesus I can do nothing, and if I have any talent it's only because he has chosen to give it to me. Be gone, in the name of Jesus.'

By the time the battle was over, so was my song. I had no idea how I'd managed to get through it. I realised that the Lord had allowed this experience so that my motives for singing in public might be tested. Whose approval did I want? Was I doing it to gain attention for myself or, as I'd promised, for his glory? I thanked him for giving me victory in this temptation and for enabling me to reject Satan's lies and recognise that I no longer needed to be accepted by men. He had made me 'accepted in the beloved' (Eph 1:6), and that was all that mattered.

That afternoon, a group of us went out onto the streets of Blackpool to share the gospel. When we'd finished, I went for a walk with a friend along the promenade, where there were horse-drawn carriages waiting to give rides to holiday-makers. The driver of one of these, seeing my guitar, shouted to us and asked me to sing him a song. I knew he was joking, but remembering that I'd promised to sing for the Lord at every opportunity, I stopped to speak to him. He had a girl in each arm and when I told him I only sang songs about Jesus, all three of them began making fun of me. Thanks to Nick's training I was no stranger to facing insults, so I stood my ground and started to sing. Almost immediately, the driver silently took his arms from around the girls and began to listen. He was obviously moved and after the song my friend and I spoke to him about the gospel. He didn't receive Christ as his Saviour there and then, but it was impossible to mistake his genuine interest, which could only be the result of God's anointing on my singing. My natural ability was nothing very special; but talent alone could never carry the truth of the gospel into a person's heart.

I remember once hearing a preacher say, 'God does little with much, much with little and everything with nothing.' The challenges I met at Blackpool may have been small ones, yet they were designed by God to impress this principle on my mind. Focusing on our own abilities leads to pride and deception; we should be less concerned with the extent of our gifts than with dedicating them, however insignificant, to the One who can do everything with our nothing. Sterner trials would come later, but in the meantime, like a soldier whose first taste of battle comes in a minor skirmish, I'd had the opportunity to prove my weapons in the face of the enemy.

It was often at a conference or convention that God spoke to me. Shortly after the Blackpool convention I went with Mum and Dad and a group from the Upper Room to a conference arranged by International Gospel Outreach (IGO), an organisation with which Mum and Dad had regular contact. While I was there, God spoke to me directly once again: 'Christine, I want you to stop watching television.'

I didn't understand why the Lord was asking this of me; after all, even Dad watched television, so why shouldn't I?

However, it wasn't necessary for me to understand, only to obey. From the moment I returned home, I avoided watching television and when Tuesday evening came round Mum and Dad were both pleased and surprised to notice me getting ready for our prayer meeting at the Upper Room. The fact was that even after being baptised in the Holy Spirit I'd never attended a single prayer meeting, excusing my absence on the grounds that I had homework to do. This was true as far as it went, but a much bigger factor was that on Tuesdays *Dallas* was on television.

But now that television was out of my life, there was nothing holding me back. I saw then why it had been necessary for the Lord to ask me to give it up; in itself it wasn't wrong, but my priorities were. Without realising it, I had neglected the commandment to love God above all else. From then on I attended prayer meetings whenever I could, even when the Lord gave me freedom to watch television again after a few months. I'd learned my lesson, and ever since I've always been careful to make sure I control my viewing habits rather than allow them to control me.

No area of life is too insignificant to be God's training ground. Minor challenges that have been overcome prepare us to meet bigger ones; a small act of obedience can give a clearer understanding of the first and great commandment. Let's not despise 'the day of small things'.

3

'Your Right Hand Shall Hold Me'

In a number of areas I had made progress as a Christian and in some ways was quite mature for my age. But there was one part of my life where quite the opposite was the case, and this was in my relationships with boys. The problem was in knowing what was the Lord's will for me, and I wasn't helped as a young teenager by receiving so much well meant advice from others in the church. It seemed that every time I formed a relationship, someone would come and tell me that this was not God's will for my life, and as I didn't want to risk stepping outside his will, I would break off the relationship, leaving the boy almost as confused as I was myself.

When I was seventeen, I started going out with Stuart and of course it wasn't long before someone told me that he wasn't the man God intended for me. The advice was more than usually unwelcome since I already felt deeply for Stuart. And besides, I could see no obvious objection to our relationship; he was eighteen – exactly a year older than me to the day – he was a member of the church and to me we seemed so well suited. I prayed and asked the Lord to show me whether the advice I'd been given was right, but my feelings made it difficult to distinguish between his will and mine and I had no assurance either way. However, my biggest fear was of failing to fulfil God's purpose for me, so the following day, in floods of tears, I told Stuart our relationship had to end. I was wretchedly unhappy.

Despite what I'd said to Stuart, I wasn't fully reconciled to losing him and continued to ask God to give me a clear indication of his will, becoming more and more bogged down in a morass of uncertainty. Eventually, Dad decided it was time to intervene, and gently suggested that I shouldn't worry so much about trying to conform to other people's ideas of God's will for me. This was sound advice which often stood me in good stead – even though in this particular case Dad was later to have cause to regret the effect of his words.

As a result, Stuart and I resumed our relationship and within a year were engaged to be married. The perfect ending; apart from just one thing. Though Dad had given his consent to our engagement, I knew he was beginning to have serious doubts about Stuart and me and was unhappy at the changes he'd seen in me. To me it seemed natural that my world should revolve around Stuart. But what Dad saw was his daughter spending virtually no time at home, neglecting her school work and giving up her plans to be a teacher in order to begin earning enough money for an early wedding.

I loved my father very much and wanted to remain close to him whether I was married or not, so I tried to set his mind at rest. I assured him that God and his will for me were more important to me than anything or anyone, even Stuart. Never thinking that I in my turn would regret what I said, I pointed out that God, knowing I wanted to please him, would sovereignly intervene to end the relationship if Stuart were not the right man for me to marry.

Having done my best to comfort Dad, I felt I could now enjoy my future prospects without a care in the world. As well as my forthcoming marriage, I saw a vista of exciting new opportunities to serve the Lord begin to open up before me. Soon after our engagement, I finished school and went to work for a large company as a trainee civil engineering technician, doing technical drawings for a power station project. Once a week I went to college to study for a HTC (Higher Technician's Certificate).

I took care not to repeat the mistake I'd made at school and on my first day at work I let everyone know I was a Christian. The company had a Christian Union, which I joined straight away. There were just four of us, out of a workforce of several hundreds, and we took it in turns to prepare a short talk, which was my first experience of expounding the word of God. I seized every opportunity to speak for the Lord in the office and was privileged to play a small part in two of the men becoming Christians.

Then there was the excitement of another FGBMFI convention at Wembley, where the speaker was to be Demos Shakarian himself, the founder of FGBMFI. I had heard Demos once before at the first British convention in Glasgow and the memory of that meeting was very precious to me because after Demos had spoken, the Lord had given me a vision that I would one day be used to minister to many people. I'd wept before the Lord, knowing I was unworthy but longing for him to use me. I went to Wembley fully expecting that he would speak to me at this convention too.

One of the speakers at Wembley related his experience of ministry in prisons and on death row. It wasn't the first time I had heard such a talk, but before I'd merely found it interesting. This time was different; I knew for certain that God was telling me that I too was going to be involved in prison ministry. It wasn't until the following day that I plucked up courage to tell anyone; I was afraid people would think I just wanted to do something sensational like the speaker the previous evening.

The first person I told was my father. 'Dad,' I said, 'the Lord has spoken to me and told me what my ministry is.'

'Oh, yes, and what's that?'

'Prison ministry.'

I half expected him to laugh. I was eighteen years old and five feet one inch tall; hardly, on the face of it, prime material for such a ministry. Dad's only response, however, was to hand me a leaflet from his inside pocket. It was all about prison ministry. He'd picked it up after the meeting the previous night.

True to his principles, Dad wouldn't interfere in what the Lord was doing and saying in my life, and nothing more was said. Sometimes I found this reticence frustrating; I trusted his wisdom, and his advice would have reassured me. But Dad knew what I really needed and always encouraged me to look to God, not man, for guidance, just as he and Mum did. And God has his own ways of preparing and directing us, often ways we don't expect.

A while after the Wembley convention, Psalm One-Fifty were invited to sing at Christian World, the largest Christian bookshop in Manchester, which ran monthly meetings for worship and teaching in its basement coffee shop. To my great surprise, the guest speaker was Noel Proctor, Chaplain of Strangeways Prison. Perhaps it was through him that I would be given a chance to begin prison ministry, I thought, so after the meeting I spoke to him about my call and asked for his advice.

His response wasn't what I expected. He suggested I should consider training as a prison officer.

'I don't mean that I feel called to minister in women's prisons,' I explained, 'but in men's.'

'Well,' he replied, 'I don't think it would really be wise for a young girl like you to be working in men's prisons.'

I was disappointed, but I couldn't blame Noel. From his point of view, his advice was sensible. He'd only just met me and I couldn't expect him there and then to share my certainty that God had spoken to me. I would just have to wait for God's time: if he had called me, he would open the right doors.

In fact, I didn't have too long to wait. One night, full of excitement, Nick called Psalm One-Fifty together to tell us that Noel had invited us to take two services at Strangeways. At Nick's request, I agreed to do a solo. As usual, I felt nervous, but I was still bound by my promise to sing for the Lord.

The day came and we were waiting in the chapel to begin the first service, which was for remand prisoners. We were all tense and keyed up, especially the girls, as the men filed in. They began eyeing us up and down and soon they were whistling and calling out to us. Their comments were unrepeatable and I could feel myself growing hot with embarrassment. I began to appreciate the soundness of Noel's earlier advice.

However, we made it through the first service and by the end we really sensed that the Spirit was at work. But we still had to face the second service for the convicted prisoners. Once again, the men filed in and we suffered a repeat performance of looks and comments, followed by whistles, clapping and stamping when Noel introduced us. When it came to my solo and I faced this cynical, jeering crowd, I prayed that the Lord would speak to them through me. My song was called 'Jesus, will you go?' and told the story of how Jesus consented to leave the splendour of heaven to die for those who would mock and spit on him. When I finished, there was complete silence. Later we had many more invitations to Strangeways and my singing was never again received in quite this way, but on this one occasion it was as if the Lord was confirming to me, and to Noel, that he wanted to use me in this ministry.

I was so happy with the way my life was going when suddenly my whole world fell apart. Without warning, Stuart broke off our engagement and I was devastated. The words I'd spoken to Dad almost a year ago now carried a bitter significance. I'd acknowledged then that God was sovereign and would end the relationship if it were wrong for me; I acknowledged it still with my mind, but it didn't make any difference to the hurt I felt. Why did God's will have to be so painful?

I revolved this question endlessly in my mind as I struggled to make sense of my shattered hopes. Had I not been too distressed to think rationally, it would have been obvious that pain is inevitable when the desires of fallen human nature have to be denied in order to conform us to the will of God – the Spirit and the flesh are constantly at war with each other and in war the loser always gets hurt.

I knew in my heart that if Stuart were not the right man for me, then God must have a plan which was even better. However, this didn't satisfy my flesh. I didn't want the 'better'. I wanted what I'd had, what Stuart and I had planned together.

To some extent, I came to terms with the situation. I had to. But in my heart a seed of rebellion was sown. I took my eyes off God's plan for me and started to make my own. In my unhappiness I began to look for something that would restore my self-esteem and make me feel better about myself. I was rather plain and always a bit over-weight, so I decided to change my appearance, make myself more attractive and, if possible, win Stuart back. I didn't recognise these intentions as rebellion – Satan is very subtle – and carried on as usual at church and in my music ministry.

My first move was to set about reducing my weight. I wouldn't need to lose much, so I didn't anticipate any big problem, and from reading magazines I already knew all the latest diet trends. I didn't actually eat a great deal to begin with: at home none of us ate breakfast and I often skipped lunch, a habit I'd acquired at school when lunch-time was taken up with sport. My main meal was in the evening and this became the target for my diet.

I knew salads and vegetables were safe, but what else? The fibre diet was popular just then and I knew I needed protein, so I thought I'd found the perfect solution when I hit on the idea of canned kidney beans. I ate a large can every day. At work I spent my breaks poring over magazine articles on diet and refusing biscuits and sweets, which, together with the fact that I wasn't really fat at all, earned me the nickname 'Podge'. Of course, I had to hide my peculiar eating habits from my family and this meant inventing excuses for eating at different times from everyone else. After a while, though, I found I couldn't completely do without sweet things and as ice cream seemed to have the fewest calories I added that to my diet too. Not being an obvious diet food, it also helped me to hide what I was doing from Mum.

However, perhaps because the rest of my diet was so unbalanced, the fat in the ice cream began to make me sick. I was actually pleased about this, as it meant I could eat more of it without gaining any weight. Satan had really deceived me in all this, though it was my rebellion which gave him the opportunity.

After a while, I was forced to admit to myself that things were getting out of control. My system became so upset by constant vomiting that my body began to reject everything I ate; even half a biscuit made me sick. I still managed somehow to keep my family in ignorance, but I couldn't fool myself any longer. I knew now that what I was doing was wrong, but I was powerless to change it. I stopped eating ice cream, but the vomiting continued. As with all sin, I'd started off in the driving seat but now I had no control over it.

My health began to suffer and I was an easy target for viruses and infections. One day I felt so ill with what I thought was flu that I couldn't go in to work. That morning I stood in the kitchen glancing over into the breakfast room where Mum was watching a chat show on television. Gradually I became transfixed by the programme as, one by one, a series of young girls described the symptoms of their illness. It all sounded dreadfully familiar: 'I used laxatives'

. . . 'I made myself vomit every day' . . . 'I never wanted to eat with the rest of the family.'

I suddenly realised that what I had wasn't flu. I had the same disease as these girls: anorexia nervosa. Some of them were literally wasting away. There were mothers, too, who told how they had lost their daughters to this modern slimmers' disease. I was horrified.

During the next few days I went through agonies. How could I do this to Mum and Dad? Stronger than ever, I felt the Holy Spirit convicting me: 'Christine, you know this is sin before me.' I did know, but I felt so helpless. Since watching that programme, I knew that facing the truth about my illness would be the first step to recovery, but then Satan would whisper: 'Do that and you know what will happen. You'll get fat again.' I would retreat in panic, thinking it was better to be ill and slim than healthy and fat, only to find myself faced once more with God's absolute demand that I repent. Finally, I surrendered to the Lord and made an appointment to see the doctor.

He was puzzled by my symptoms, as little was known then about anorexia and even less about bulimia, but when I told him about the girls I'd seen on television he immediately arranged for me to see a specialist.

When I kept the appointment, I was astounded to discover that the specialist was actually a psychiatrist who, after asking a lot of questions, began trying to convince me that my problem was due to an unhappy home and family life. Nothing could have been further from the truth and I knew that this man couldn't help me. As soon as I could, I escaped, resolving never to go back. It was just me and the Lord now, I thought.

The vomiting got worse over the next few weeks, but then I was given another appointment with a different doctor – completely different, in fact. This one spent time putting me at ease and then just listened as I described my symptoms. He made no judgements, and when I'd finished, as I'd expected, he confirmed that I had anorexia.

But he insisted that next time I saw him Mum had to come too, and he would tell her the truth.

Between then and the next appointment I ate less than ever, worrying about how Mum would react. I hated myself for doing this to her. So far, she only knew I was having trouble digesting food, which was all I'd been able to tell her.

Too soon for me, the day of the appointment came. The journey to the hospital was a nightmare, and then we were sitting in the doctor's office as he pronounced the words I'd dreaded. 'Mrs Hailes, your daughter has anorexia nervosa.'

I looked at Mum. Her face registered total horror and disbelief. She didn't hear a word the doctor was saying about his plans for my treatment.

Afterwards, I tried to comfort her: I would be visiting the hospital weekly as an outpatient and my decision to seek help was a sign of my determination to get better. As I said this, I felt a faint twinge of uneasiness. However, I kept all my appointments. (This, of course, meant I had to tell people at the office about my anorexia, in order to explain my absences, but I told very few others.) Between appointments, I had to write down everything I ate, which in fact resulted in my eating less, as I couldn't be bothered to write down 'half a biscuit' or 'a bite of Mum's apple'. It was easier to cut them out.

The goodness of God is amazing. Though my eating habits were no better at all, I noticed my weight never once went below 7st 2lb. This was a miracle, as I was eating much less than other girls who weighed 5st, and was vomiting what little I did eat. It was clear evidence that the Lord was upholding me throughout this ordeal. I marvelled at his faithfulness to me in the face of my rejection of his will. I found, like the psalmist, that I couldn't run away from the loving hand of God:

Where can I go from Your Spirit? Or where can I flee from Your presence? If I ascend into heaven, You are there; if I make my bed in hell, behold, You are there. If I take the wings of the morning, and dwell in the uttermost parts of the sea, even there Your hand shall lead me, and Your right hand shall hold me (Ps 139:7–10).

Even in my rebellion, he was there all the time. He didn't give up on me; even more, he was still prepared to use me.

4

'Are You Willing?'

A visiting missionary speaker at the Upper Room was nothing unusual. We had them often, and one of the most frequent and popular visitors was the Revd David Nellist. David was an independent travelling preacher and evangelist, well known and respected in International Gospel Outreach circles and among the many people who went to the Hollybush camps in North Yorkshire. Since the late 1970s, he had been making short missionary visits to the Philippines a couple of times a year, working among tribal groups such as the Negritos and Aetas. His vision was to train Filipino converts to evangelise their own nation and he had established a work in the village of Cabalan in the Subic Bay area of Luzon, which is the largest of the Philippine islands.

As David's own ministry took him all over the world, the work in Calaban was staffed permanently by two other English missionaries, one of whom, Dorothy, came with him to the Upper Room one weekend in the spring of 1983. I watched and listened while Dorothy spoke about the work and showed her slides. I was interested and impressed, but nothing more. Then David stood up to preach. As usual, he gave a powerful challenge concerning the urgent need for foreign missions – but that was for other people, I thought. I was happy with the prison ministry I already had and was visiting prisons fairly regularly by now with Psalm One-Fifty; we had just made an album and were receiving plenty of invitations.

At the end of his talk, David made an appeal: 'If you are willing to go to the foreign mission field to serve the Lord, I want you to step forward tonight. I'm not saying that you will certainly go, but are you willing?'

At that moment, the Lord spoke to me. I knew that he was calling me, not simply to be willing but, clearly and definitely, actually to go to the Philippines. How many times in the past had it been easy just to say, 'Yes, Lord'? But not this time. I loved and feared the Lord too much to say 'no', yet I couldn't bring myself to submit to this request.

A few people began to get up and go to the front. I huddled in my chair, wishing that the ground would swallow me up, and hoping desperately that no one was looking at me. I was sure that guilt and embarrassment must be written all over my face for anyone to see. I couldn't wait for the service to finish and stayed rigidly in my seat until it was all over. Afterwards, I quickly started talking to my friends about other things in an effort to take my mind off what the Lord had asked. Though I couldn't say 'no', neither could I say 'yes', so I fought to avoid answering at all. It would be a relief to get back to work, where I wouldn't have to think about it. Or so I thought.

Next day, at the office, I discovered my mistake. The Lord wasn't to be put off; he wanted an answer, and I had to make a choice. Doggedly, I tried to concentrate on my work and refused to commit myself. I survived Monday, but Tuesday was worse. Instead of my drawings, all I could see were Filipinos running off the edge of a cliff into a Christless eternity. The Lord's voice was insistent: 'Christine, they need you to tell them.'

I thought about my present ministry, and how much I enjoyed it; I didn't want to give it up, even for a little while.

Then I tried to imagine myself working among primitive tribes. How could the Lord ask this of me? What about the prison ministry he'd given me? I tried another tack. 'Lord,' I said, 'I've never been to Bible school; and what do I know about preaching?'

'Christine, all I'm asking you to do is love the people. Can you love the people?'

This cut through all my evasions and defences. It was the sort of question my dad had a knack of asking. I began to see where he got it from. It put me in a no-win situation. If I said 'no', I'd be denying the power of the Holy Spirit within me. I'd often sung a song based on Romans 5:5 and knew very well the truth that 'the love of God has been poured out in our hearts by the Holy Spirit who was given to us'. But if I said 'yes' . . . .

'Yes, Lord. I can love the people. I surrender.' I put down my draughting pen and made an announcement to the lads in the office: 'Guess where I'm going!'

'Where are you off to now then, Podge?' asked Norman, obviously expecting me to tell him about one of my prison visits.

'The Philippines. God's called me to go there.'

'Come on, Podge! Don't be stupid! You can't even eat in England, let alone the Philippines. You'll end up coming back in a box, and I'm not buying flowers.'

With everything else on my mind, I hadn't thought about my anorexia which, despite all my visits to the hospital, was still no better. Somehow, though, it didn't seem important. 'If God has called me, then he'll heal me,' I said.

'What about money, then?' Norman asked. He knew I'd been struggling to find the money for my summer holiday in Spain with friends from church.

'If God wants me to go, he'll provide what I need.'

'But where will you stay when you get there?'

By now, he must have been anticipating my answer. 'God will give me somewhere to live.'

The others in the office remained silent, listening intently. They could tell I meant what I said. I hadn't spoken lightly and there was no doubt in my mind that God was going to meet all my needs – even though I would have preferred him not to.

When I got home that evening, I told my parents. They didn't say much, which didn't surprise me. I knew them well enough by now not to expect them either to approve or try to dissuade me. Straight afterwards, I phoned David Nellist, as he was my only contact with the Philippines, to ask for his help. At this time, I had one more year of my HTC course to complete, so I told David that I'd like to spend the summer, while college was closed, working in the Philippines. However, he explained that summer wouldn't be a suitable time to go, because it would be the rainy season, when the work was often hampered by the rains and even fierce storms and typhoons. His advice was that it would be better to go in September.

It dawned on me at this point that I had never even asked the Lord how long I was to stay in the Philippines. I had just assumed it would be a month or two. But if I were to take David's advice and go in September, I would have to miss college, and in that case I might as well take the opportunity to stay for ten months until the next rainy season and pick up at college the following September. When I told David what I was thinking, he invited me to become part of his own small mission, working alongside Dorothy and her colleague, Linda.

So within a day everything was settled: I would be flying out to the Philippines in just three or four months' time. Not long afterwards, someone asked me, 'Where are the Philippines, anyway?' It came over me afresh just how little concrete planning I'd done; I didn't even know exactly where I was going. I went to find a map. 'Australia, up a bit, left a bit,' I answered.

I didn't know anything about this place. At this point I still thought it was populated entirely by tribal peoples, as it was with these that David's mission was particularly concerned. But now that I'd committed myself I was no longer troubled by this prospect; I was willing to go wherever the Lord sent me. Only two things remained to be sorted out: my fare and my anorexia. God dealt with my anorexia first.

A few weeks later, I attended a FGBMFI breakfast meeting, where the speaker was Allan Jones. After he had given his testimony, he began to speak out some words of knowledge which the Holy Spirit had revealed to him. 'There's someone here with a serious digestion problem.'

'Gosh,' I thought, 'that's what I used to call my anorexia.'

'If you will come out to the front here this morning,' Allan went on, 'God will heal you.'

I knew this word of knowledge was for me. And then the full significance of it hit me: God would heal me *if I went out to the front*. He was requiring something of me. Satan, as ever, was there immediately, trying to sow confusion and tempting me to disobedience with the same words he'd used before: 'If you do that, you'll get fat.'

I recognised this temptation for what it was, but I really didn't want to get fat. I couldn't make myself go forward; I felt as if my feet were glued to the carpet. In a moment of painful insight, it became clear to me that although I'd thought my willingness to go to the doctor was a step towards recovery, the truth was that I didn't want to get better. I wanted this illness because it kept me slim.

Then the Lord spoke to me, very solemnly and sternly: 'Christine, it's now or never.'

I felt as if I'd been brought out of a daze by a blow in the face. I knew that it was only by God's grace and forbearance that my weight had so far never fallen below 7st 2lb; and now he had delivered an ultimatum. If I continued in rebellion, he would withdraw his protection, the anorexia would run its course and I would lose my life. But still I stayed rooted to the spot. And then I remembered my commitment to the mission in the Philippines. If I jeopardised my health it would be impossible for me to go. By refusing to be healed I was in effect going back on my promise.

At that, I quickly shuffled my way to the front and joined the others already standing there in response to other words of knowledge that Allan had given. Allan prayed for us all and though I felt nothing, I knew in my heart that I'd stopped rebelling against God. I was utterly free. I went home and ate a good meal, and for the first time in almost a year I didn't have to go to the bathroom afterwards to vomit. From that time, the vomiting stopped and I never went back to the hospital. I was completely healed.

That left the other problem – my fare. I was well aware that Dad wouldn't pay. In accordance with his principle of never interfering in my dealings with the Lord, he would expect me to look to God to confirm his call by supplying my needs. And God's confirmation was particularly important this time – we've always been a very close family, and Mum and Dad hated the thought of us being separated just as much as I did. They wouldn't offer me any encouragement in a venture which would take me thousands of miles away unless it was undeniably the Lord's will. I would simply have to pray about it.

My prayers were answered on my twenty-first birthday, which fell on 15th June 1983. Mum had organised a party for me with all our friends at church and I was really touched by all the love and kindness everyone showed me. I had so many lovely gifts, most of which had been chosen with the Philippines in mind. There were suitcases and sundresses, and one lady, Alice, had decorated my cake with a plane flying away from a map of England.

Then one of the couples in the church, David and Anne, slipped an envelope into my hand as they wished me a happy birthday. It contained £500 – more than enough for a return ticket – which the Lord had told David to give me. I knew then that although I would have no fixed income while I was away I could trust the Lord to provide for me. (And in fact, although I hadn't asked for financial support, the congregation at the Upper Room subsequently decided to take up a special collection for me once a month.)

Mum and I almost cried our way through the next two months; we could hardly bear the prospect of being apart for almost a year. How little we knew! If we'd realised then what the future held, neither of us could have coped. By now I was totally secure in the fact that this step was the Lord's will, but he graciously gave us many words of encouragement and confirmation during those two months.

Another blessing I hadn't counted on was a companion for the journey. Through Jonathan, who had been working as co-pastor with Dad at the Upper Room, I was put in touch with a girl called Lesley Keenan. Lesley was due to fly out to work as a nurse with a mission based in the same part of the Philippines as David's (though not connected with it). We booked our flights to Manila for the same day in September.

Shortly before I was due to leave, David Chaudhary, a missionary and preacher whom my parents knew through their contact with International Gospel Outreach, prayed for me, asking the Lord to give me favour with the authorities. It struck me as an odd thing to pray for; what 'authorities' would I encounter in a tribal situation? But I stored it away to meditate on.

On the day of my flight, after a painful parting from the rest of the family, Dad drove me to the airport with Mum and Nanna Jean. We cried throughout the entire journey. Even Dad's vision must have been blurred by a tear or two, because we suddenly realised we were heading for the wrong airport; we were on the way to Heathrow, and my plane was departing from Gatwick.

'Gatwick?' yelled Dad. 'We'll never make it.' Suddenly,

the problem of getting there on time pushed everything else into the background. We arrived at Gatwick with only minutes to spare. In a way it was a good thing that we were so late; there was no time for long, tearful goodbyes – nor was there time to weigh my luggage, which was hugely over the limit, with my guitar, books, Bibles, clothes, teddy bears and a good stock of my favourite chocolate.

After a brief farewell, I had to hurry straight onto the plane, and thankfully took my seat next to Lesley. She was about my age and I could tell that she too was upset at leaving her family, so we waited until our emotions had subsided a bit before starting to chat to each other. We hadn't been in the air very long when a stewardess came up to me.

'Are you Christine Hailes?' she asked. I immediately thought something awful had happened to Mum and Dad.

'Yes,' I replied, apprehensively.

'You dropped your passport at Gatwick. What do you want to do? Do you want to disembark at Frankfurt or take a risk and go on to Manila?'

I realised she needed an immediate decision, and I found that I was able to answer, as calmly as if she'd asked where I wanted to take my tea, 'Um, I think I'll just go on to Manila, thank you.'

As I sat there, I laid the problem before the Lord. 'Lord, it's all up to you now. You'll have to find a way of getting me into the Philippines without a passport.' With that, I left it in his hands.

'How long do you plan to stay in the Philippines?' Lesley asked.

'Just ten months.'

'Gosh,' she exclaimed, 'how can you manage that long?'

'I don't really know. The Lord will have to do something. How about you?'

'Only six months,' she replied, little knowing that her future too contained some surprises. Fourteen years later, she is still ministering in the Philippines.

After a seemingly endless twenty-one-hour flight we finally arrived in Manila. Getting there, however, was the easy part; my problem was going to be staying there without a passport. As I queued at immigration I prayed, 'Well, Lord, you've got me this far, and I trust you to get me through this.'

'Passport, please, miss.'

The immigration officer listened carefully as I explained what had happened and then disappeared for several minutes, asking me to wait. Lesley went on ahead while I continued to pray quietly. When the officer returned he was accompanied by several others who were obviously of higher rank. I went through my story again and one of them left to make a phone call. They all seemed very grave and it was plain that they were considering asking me to take the first plane back to England. I discovered later that security was particularly tight just then; only three weeks earlier, Benigno Aquino, the chief political rival of the President, Ferdinand Marcos, had been shot dead at that very airport. Had I but known it, I was entering a country which at that time was beset by political strife, instability and other evils resulting in large part from Marcos' repressive regime.

However, still happily ignorant of all this, I waited again. I knew that the God I believed in was a God who specialised in doing things which seemed impossible, but it was still with a profound sense of relief that I eventually heard that my passport was already in transit and that provided I returned to collect it in a few days' time permission had been granted to allow me through. 'Thank you, Lord!'

I was finally able to rejoin Lesley, whom I found patiently waiting along with Dorothy, who had come to meet me. The three of us were staying overnight together in Manila. On the short taxi-ride to our hotel, I was too exhausted to do more than register the fact that, at least here in the capital, I wasn't in an undeveloped tribal area.

And the hotel itself was as luxurious as anything I'd encountered in England.

Comfortable as it was, though, I didn't spend much time sleeping that night, in spite of my tiredness. I was sharing a room with Lesley and Dorothy and, not wanting to disturb them by switching on the light, I spent several hours in the bathroom writing letters home. I was already homesick and I couldn't hold back my tears. Reflected in the mirror I saw a twenty-one-year-old girl clutching a teddy bear and crying for her mother.

'What can the Lord possibly do with me?' I thought. 'Can he really have a purpose for me here?'

5

'I Was in Prison and You Came to Me'

Next morning we said goodbye to Lesley, who was flying north to Baguio City on the way to join her mission in San Fernando. Dorothy and I were also going north, but by road up the west coast of Luzon to Subic Bay. We had a long journey ahead of us, which began with a taxi-ride to the bus station. As we climbed into the taxi, I thought privately that it looked ready to fall apart, but I said nothing, not wanting to betray my inexperience. As soon as we set off, I realised why the taxi was in such a state. 'He drives this thing into the ground,' I said to Dorothy.

'Oh, Chrissy, this is nothing. Wait until he really gets going!'

As we drove, I began to get a fuller picture of Manila. A few minutes away from the opulent area around the hotel, we encountered one of the hundreds of shanty towns which house the poorer section of the population. I'd never seen real poverty before and nothing had prepared me for this. Of course, I'd seen television documentaries about third-world poverty, but the images of blue skies and sunshine, so attractive to English eyes, had distracted me from the grim reality. And besides, television reaches only two of the five senses. Here, I could actually experience the intense heat that these people were living in and feel my energy draining away in the humid atmosphere. The smell was nauseating; there were piles of garbage anywhere and everywhere. Half-dressed toddlers were wandering around unsupervised, while older children scurried in and out of the traffic trying to sell anything from sweets and cigarettes to floor mats. When the traffic halted, small children would lead their blind or disabled parents from car to car, knocking on the windows and begging for money.

The moving traffic was absolutely chaotic. It made London in the rush hour seem like a quiet Cornish village. Though there were only four lanes officially, the drivers managed to squeeze in another two, recklessly weaving from one to another at frightening speed. Ancient buses billowed out dense black fumes which, combined with the stifling heat, made it almost impossible to breathe. 'How can people live and work in these conditions?' I asked myself.

Manila is a city of extremes; alongside the starkest poverty lies the evidence of immense wealth. Beyond the shanty town I saw shopping malls larger than anything I'd encountered before, as well as enormous, imposing skyscrapers and exquisite houses. My preconceived ideas of the Philippines as a country at a tribal stage of development were undergoing a rapid readjustment.

In actual fact, the process of modernisation under western influence began as long ago as the sixteenth century, when the Philippines became a Spanish colony; it was accelerated from the end of the nineteenth when America took over the islands from Spain. One lasting result of Spanish influence is that most Filipinos are (nominally at least) Roman Catholic. Full independence was gained in 1946 (though America maintained military bases in the Philippines until 1992). The economy is both agricultural and industrial but it has been badly disrupted by political and social unrest, resulting in widespread poverty and unemployment. The tribal peoples, who I'd thought made up the whole population, really make up less than three per cent!

When we got out of the taxi at the bus station we were immediately surrounded by a crowd of men, all insisting loudly that they would carry our luggage. I thought it was very kind of them and was surprised when Dorothy refused so firmly. She explained later that the men, taking us for rich American ladies, would expect to be handsomely rewarded for helping us – and there was a strong chance of losing an item or two if we lost control of our things.

The coach which was to take us as far as Olongapo, 120 miles to the north, was comfortable and air-conditioned, and for the next four hours I slid back into the world I knew. It was like watching those television programmes, observing without feeling. During the long, quiet journey, homesickness began to creep over me again, but I cheered up as we neared Olongapo and the road began to climb. The country was hilly and green and reminded me of the Welsh village where my parents had their holiday home.

At last Dorothy announced that we were actually in Olongapo City. 'This is a city?' I thought. 'It looks more like a big shanty town.' There seemed to be no pattern or order to anything. There were open-front car workshops, bakeries and a market place all crowded together, and shops whose window displays were so crammed and chaotic you could hardly make out what was for sale. Everything looked grey and dirty, even though the sun was shining.

However, there was no time to look around. We still had another six or seven miles to travel to Subic Town, our final destination. On this last stage of our journey we rode in a jeepney, which is the most common form of public transport in the Philippines and resembles an elongated, open-sided, windowless jeep embellished with highly coloured decorations and providing bench seating for about sixteen passengers. There are no predetermined stopping points; the jeepney stops to pick up passengers or allow them to alight anywhere along the route. After about half an hour, Dorothy called out to the driver: '*Para na ho*' ('Stop now, please') and the jeepney screeched to a halt.

'Chrissy, we're home now.'

Home. For the next ten months I'd have to get used to thinking of Subic as 'home'. Still entertaining the notion that I was destined to work in a tribal situation, I'd been surprised, when we first entered Subic, to find myself in such a built-up area. It had been a pleasant surprise, however, because this promised a less drastic change of life style than I'd anticipated.

Subic is a small coastal town with a population of about 60,000, one of several towns and cities which together form the Subic Bay area. My first impression was that it had a curiously half-finished appearance, which was due to the fact that the inhabitants had to build and develop their houses at a pace dictated by their limited incomes. Even a completed house might remain unpainted or unglazed for ages. It was a bit like a huge building site. Everywhere there were heaps of rubbish, especially in the area by the shore, right next to the market; this presented an odd contrast to the people themselves, who all looked so clean.

I'd been surprised, too, to notice a number of American GIs walking around. I hadn't realised there was a large US naval base nearby in Olongapo. I was less surprised, after experiencing the shanty town in Manila, to see so many blind and disabled beggars sitting in the streets, or to observe the street kids hanging around waiting for small jobs.

Dorothy and I got out of the jeepney and I found myself in front of a row of small terraced houses situated in a fenced area known as a compound. Out of the house at the end of the row came two young women, one English and one Filipina, who ran to meet us and help us with our bags. I was introduced to Linda, Dorothy's missionary colleague, and Redemia, their helper and interpreter. Redemia was a Negrito (one of the minority tribal groups). She was tiny –

less than five feet tall – and extremely pretty, with long crinkly hair and skin much darker than the more common brown of the majority of Filipinos.

They led us into the house and from bright sunlight I was plunged into what seemed like total darkness. Too many windows were not a good idea, I was told, as they let in heat as well as light. I saw the point of this when Linda took me upstairs to see the two small bedrooms, which in the daytime were very light but almost unbearably hot. Dorothy and Linda wanted to give me the most comfortable bed, but eventually I persuaded them that Redemia and I, being several years younger than they, should take the metal-framed bunks in the smaller room, where there was just space also for a wardrobe (and, as I later discovered, a rat).

Downstairs again, Dorothy decided to take a shower and disappeared into the bathroom next to the kitchen. 'Kitchen' is perhaps a bit of an overstatement, as the ground floor was an open-plan area with a tiled work top and a sink in one corner. Under the sink was a small cupboard for pans – and cockroaches (which proved impossible to eliminate, despite Dorothy's insistence on meticulous attention to cleanliness); on the wall was another small cupboard for cockroaches and cans, etc. The cooker was a Calor gas camping stove.

The rest of the furniture was just as basic: a Formica-topped table, a very small plastic-covered sofa, a couple of hard chairs, a chest of drawers and a small black and white television. As in many ordinary houses in the Philippines, the floor was of cement and was painted red.

Dorothy emerged from the shower and I took my turn in the tiny bathroom. Again, I saw that 'bathroom' was something of a misnomer, as there was no bath – only rich people have baths in the Philippines – just a toilet, a wash basin and the 'shower', which consisted of a shower head sticking out of the wall. The water obviously drained away through a grid in the floor. 'Ah, well,' I thought, 'it could be worse.' Then the truth hit me. There was no hot water.

I'd never taken a cold shower in my life, not even after a hard game of squash. Hesitantly, I turned on the tap and flinched at the temperature of the water. 'No hot water! No bath! How can I bear it?' I muttered. Then, reminding myself that I ought to be grateful that we had running water at all, I gritted my teeth and shivered through my shower.

And really, cold showers began to assume the character of a minor inconvenience when I learned what Dorothy and Linda had endured in the past. Once I'd unpacked and settled in, it was time for me to catch up on their news and assess the situation; circumstances had changed since that weekend earlier in the year when Dorothy came with David to speak at the Upper Room. The work Dorothy had described on that occasion was based in Cabalan, a village just south of Olongapo. The hills surrounding the village were populated by tribal peoples whom Dorothy and Linda would visit regularly, travelling miles on foot and preaching the gospel as they went. Those who responded were invited to Dorothy's home for Bible school training every day. Redemia had been one of their students and had progressed so well that David had sponsored her through a further course at a Bible school in Manila.

Dorothy had moved into Cabalan alone five years previously. Before that, she had spent a year in the Philippines with another mission and at the end of it she'd felt a strong desire to return. David, whose wife was a close friend of Dorothy, had been able to enlist the help of a local pastor in Cabalan, whom he'd met on one of his own missionary visits. This pastor had helped Dorothy set up the work and had provided her with accommodation. Linda had joined her a couple of years later, having received a call to the Philippines after hearing David speak at the Bible college in Scotland where she was studying.

Together they continued the work, seeing many converts among the Aetas and Negritos who, through the teaching they received in the small Bible school, were firmly established in their Christian faith. (Today, a number of them are conducting successful ministries in evangelism and pastoral work among their own people.) Then suddenly, without warning, the local pastor asked them to leave their accommodation and they were forced to move into a rented house, made of wood and full of rats and termites and without running water. For a while they struggled on with the Bible school, but finally the house became impossible to live in and the school had to close. Dorothy and Linda were then faced with the need to rent new accommodation in time for my arrival and had only just settled in Subic themselves. Our present house, they assured me, was luxurious compared to their previous one.

As I listened, I felt very privileged to be able to walk straight into a situation where all the practical arrangements had been made and where I could draw on Dorothy's and Linda's experience. I particularly admired Dorothy; I couldn't imagine myself being able to start from scratch, all alone, as she did.

Having hurried to prepare a place for me, Dorothy and Linda had had no time to consider their own future plans. But at David's request, they had made some preliminary enquiries and arrangements on my behalf. Having learned from David of my prison ministry in England, Dorothy had contacted one of the local jails and received permission for us to visit.

I remembered how my dismay at the thought of giving up my prison ministry had made me so reluctant to come to the Philippines; how I'd questioned God's ways in opening up this ministry for me only to call me to do something entirely different, as I'd thought, halfway across the world. I saw now that though God's purposes are not always clear to us, we can trust him to work them out in our lives. I'd thought my prison ministry and my call to the Philippines were mutually exclusive, yet here I was, about to visit a Philippine prison.

Not immediately, however. I'd arrived at the tail-end of the rainy season and for a couple of weeks the bad weather returned, making it impossible to venture far from the house. This gave me the opportunity to recover from jet lag and familiarise myself with my immediate neighbourhood.

As the house was part of a terrace, we were very close to our neighbours. In fact, two steps out of the front door and we were already in the next house! Most of the houses in the compound were owned by members of one extended family, one of whom was our landlord. Some of them were very poor, others rather better off, but all were friendly and later we got to know many of them quite well.

At the back of the compound was a small piggery and beyond that a boggy area of stagnant water where I was amazed to see children swimming. You didn't have to walk far before encountering a rubbish heap – a circumstance which rather undermined our own efforts to maintain hygienic surroundings. Mice, and even rats, proved an ineradicable problem. The mice didn't even wait for us to finish a meal before appearing to claim their share. Bowing to the inevitable, we ended, like Cinderella in the Disney film, by making friends with them. I never got used to the rats, though.

Right alongside us was the Municipal Hall, the equivalent of a Town Hall, where the mayor's office, the post office and Subic Jail (not the one we were due to visit) were located.

Eventually better weather arrived, and with it the moment I'd been waiting for – the day of our first visit to the jail. Camp Maquinaya was a fifteen-minute jeepney ride from our house, on the road to Olongapo. It was a Friday morning when the four of us – Dorothy, Linda,

Redemia and I – set off, none of us having very much idea of what awaited us.

We presented ourselves at the padlocked gate, which was opened for us by a police officer who had a desk by the entrance (prison officers are also police officers in the Philippines) and we were led into a compound surrounded by a barbed-wire fence. Within the compound were two separate cell blocks called Alpha and Bravo. The officer indicated a spot in the compound where we could hold an open-air service and then left us to return to his desk.

Security seemed very lax, the barbed-wire fence being the only apparent barrier to escape. Later, we understood prison security better. Escape attempts were few because all the guards were armed and would simply shoot anyone who tried it. A warden once remarked to me concerning a particular prisoner: 'This inmate's mother was very grateful to me. When her son tried to escape, I ordered him to be shot in the leg. Others would have given orders to kill.'

I looked round the compound. This was nothing like Strangeways. No chapel, no seats, no organ; and above all, no guards to ensure our safety. We soon learned that the guards remain outside the jail most of the time and that visitors who enter do so at their own risk. To all outward appearances we were at the mercy of the prisoners.

In the late 1980s, the world was horrified by the news that a group of western missionaries had been raped and murdered in a Philippine jail in Davao City on the island of Mindanao. The news prompted many people to ask me whether I was ever afraid to minister in the jails. I always replied that every time I went in, I went with the assurance that my life was not in the hands of the inmates, nor in my own, but in God's. I know that no harm can come to me unless God allows it; and should he allow it, then I believe that it will be ultimately for my good. 'All things work together for good to those who love God' (Rom 8:28);

and 'whether we live or die, we are the Lord's' (Rom 14:8).

I picked up my guitar and started to play. Immediately, a group of inmates began to gather round us and as we sang some of them even tried to join in. After the singing, we gave a simple gospel message which Redemia translated into Tagalog, the local dialect of the area and also the main national language of the Philippines. Dorothy knew quite a lot of Tagalog, but wasn't fluent enough to preach, and though English is the second national language, many uneducated people can't understand it at all; and of course, the jails contain a high percentage of uneducated people. But they all listened intently to every word and at the end we were thrilled when a number of them professed a desire to accept Christ as Lord and Saviour.

After the service, some of them invited us inside their cells. This would remove us even further from the possibility of help but, not wanting to rebuff their overtures of friendship, we accepted. Within the cell blocks there was no individual accommodation, just large communal cells. The inmates had secured a measure of privacy for themselves by constructing bedroom areas out of papier-mâché and string. For wallpaper, they used old magazines and newspapers. Though one or two had folding sun-loungers or bare wooden beds, most had no beds at all. There was no running water and no toilets.

Nevertheless, they were eager to show us what hospitality they could and bought us soda and crackers from the prison tuck shop, and while we ate and drank they began to talk about their lives. They all wore civilian clothes, for the most part completely threadbare. They were given no clothes, they explained, nor any soap or toothpaste. If their families were unable to supply these necessities, they either had to do without or find some way of earning a little money to buy them. These conditions apply in jails throughout the Philippines and in each the inmates try to develop skills in various crafts, producing artefacts which are offered for sale to visitors. In Camp Maquinaya, it was mostly woodcarving. The tiny income this generates also enables them to supplement the low quality prison diet with food from the vendors who visit daily.

We were staggered to learn that many of the men had endured these conditions for up to ten years without yet having been convicted. Like almost all Philippine jails, Camp Maquinaya was a remand prison. After conviction and sentencing, prisoners were transferred to the main prison in the Muntinlupa district of Manila; any who were acquitted would receive no compensation for the years spent in jail.

The majority of Camp Maquinaya's inmates were being held on charges of murder or drug-related offences, and while their guilt or innocence had yet to be established, there was no doubt that we were in the presence of men who were capable of hideous violence. The two cell blocks Alpha and Bravo reflected the need to separate two rival gangs among the inmates, between whom existed the bitterest rivalry and hostility. Given the opportunity, this might at any time erupt into violence and it was not unknown for quarrels arising from the most trivial causes to end in murder.

One visit was more than enough to confirm to us that the grace of God alone could bring light into this dark place. There was a work for us here. The warden in charge of the jail raised no objection to our request to visit every Friday, and this became part of our normal schedule.

Life began to assume a regular pattern. On Sundays, of course, we went to church. Dorothy, Linda, Redemia and I all attended an Assemblies of God church in Olongapo, where Dorothy taught adult Sunday school. The congregation of about 100 members were of all ages and were mainly Filipino, though quite a number of US military service men and women also attended as the pastor spoke excellent English. The sermons were given in 'Taglish', a mixture of Tagalog and English.

A month or so after our first visit to Camp Maquinaya, we obtained permission to visit the small jail in Subic Town. As this was situated in the Municipal Hall next to our house, the inmates were literally our neighbours. Every Monday night we conducted services for them along similar lines to those at Camp Maquinaya. This growing prison work had been initiated as a result of my own previous experience, but the other three girls were unstinting in their efforts to promote what was to them a very different area of ministry from the one they had known before.

Almost unwittingly, we also found ourselves developing a ministry to the children of Subic. Redemia had a beautiful voice and she and I would often sit outside the house singing together as I played my guitar. I've always found a guitar to be an effective crowd puller and we quickly gathered an audience of local children. It seemed natural to speak to them about the gospel, and before long all four of us were involved in organising simple Bible instruction for them every Thursday afternoon. Very soon we moved further afield and began children's outreaches in other *barangays* (village-like subdivisions) of Subic Town. I'd only just started to learn Tagalog with Redemia, so mostly all I could offer was my guitar, a song and a smile: just loving the kids.

Linda felt a particular call to the children's work and she began to head up this side of our ministry. The work nearest my own heart was the prison ministry. Our visits were a real source of joy to me and before long I found myself going along on my own, aside from our scheduled services, just to spend time with the inmates. At their request I helped them learn the songs we sang in the services and bought them a guitar so that they could participate themselves. From being my ministry, they were becoming my friends.

Later, when I'd had more experience, I realised that Camp Maquinaya was one of the worst jails in the Philippines. On some occasions, while we were holding a service in one room, other inmates who didn't attend the services were having a drunken orgy in the next cell. Alcohol, drugs and prostitutes were all available at a price. Guards would turn a blind eye – but expected to be rewarded in return.

Gradually I became involved in helping the inmates in other ways. Several of them asked me to lend moral support by being there in court when their hearings came up, or by accompanying them on visits to their lawyers. One of these was Rhey. He was the 'mayor' of Alpha group (the mayor was the acknowledged leader of the group and commanded unquestioned obedience). Rhey was one of the most hardened criminals in the jail yet, such is the grace of God, he was also one of the most responsive to the gospel. His conversion, which was deep and lasting, was one of my greatest encouragements. As a Christian he retained the respect of the other inmates and his habit of command. I learned later that the reason our services were so well attended when he was mayor was that he made attendance compulsory.

I'd never questioned him about his criminal record. I decided right from the start that I would always wait for a prisoner to confide in me. So when I first went with him to a court hearing I received a shock. Rhey had killed a man with a pair of scissors. But shock was quickly swallowed up by compassion. Many of the inmates were guilty of horrific crimes, but the reason I had come to the Philippines was to reach out to those who were rushing headlong down the road to destruction, and to tell them of their need for a Saviour.

I thought back to the time when I was still working as a technician and my colleague Norman had questioned me about my prison work in England: 'Why do you waste your time on a bunch of convicts when there are people so much more deserving?'

But isn't it good that God doesn't give us what we deserve? If he did, none of us would have any hope. We're all sinners dependent on his mercy: 'But God demonstrates

His own love toward us, in that while we were still sinners, Christ died for us' (Rom 5:8). The recognition of my own unworthiness was sufficient reason for not rejecting Rhey.

The passage of Scripture which spurred me on perhaps more than any other was the parable of the sheep and the goats. To those who inherit the kingdom of heaven, Jesus says:

> I was naked and you clothed Me; I was sick and you visited Me; I was in prison and you came to Me . . . Assuredly, I say to you, inasmuch as you did it to one of the least of these My brethren, you did it to Me (Mt 25:36, 40).

6

Eddie

Almost before I knew it, Christmas was approaching and inevitably my mind turned towards home. I thought about the huge family celebration I'd be missing this year and a great wave of homesickness swept over me as I contemplated the prospect of spending Christmas so far away from those I loved.

I was rescued from these gloomy introspections by the realisation that, in the prison inmates who had come to mean so much to me, I had a family right here in the Philippines. I remembered too that a large part of my mother's preparations for Christmas consisted of ensuring that every poor family she knew received a gift on Christmas day. What could I do to make Christmas special for the inmates? Unlike British prisoners, who are provided with entertainment and a traditional Christmas dinner, inmates in the Philippines would spend Christmas day much like any other.

My first thought was to do some baking, but on a Calor gas stove that was impossible. I couldn't afford to buy gifts for all the inmates and it wouldn't be fair to single out a few. Materially, there was little I could do. I decided to ask the youth group at the church we attended in Olongapo if they would be willing to take part in a special service at

Camp Maquinaya just before Christmas. None of them had ever been inside a jail before and not unnaturally some found the idea daunting. Nevertheless, they all agreed and together we began to devise a programme of good Christian Christmas songs and a short narration of the nativity story.

As I immersed myself in the preparations I found myself eagerly looking forward to Christmas instead of dreading it, as I pictured to myself the inmates' pleasure at seeing such a large party of young people. I solved the problem of presents by buying a big tin of biscuits for each of the cell groups, as well as a few small gifts for one of the inmates who was being transferred to Muntinlupa. The 23rd December was going to be a truly special day.

A week before the Christmas presentation, Dorothy, Linda, Redemia and I paid our usual Friday visit to Camp Maquinaya. Attendance at the service was unusually low that morning, and I was particularly surprised by Eddie Lazaro's absence. It wasn't like Eddie to miss a service; he'd been one of the first to respond to the word of God and I'd been greatly encouraged by his spiritual progress. He'd developed a genuine friendship with all four of us and often referred to me as his adopted sister. The reason for the absences was explained by one of the other inmates, who told me that a large group had been summoned to attend court hearings. Things were moving pretty fast in Eddie's case: he'd only been in the jail for six months. He was being held on a murder charge but consistently maintained that he hadn't intended to kill his victim and was hoping that the charge would be reduced to manslaughter.

During the closing part of the service the absentees returned. As they were led through the gate I saw Eddie, his face split by an enormous smile. The whispered news spread rapidly: Eddie had been completely acquitted.

We finished the service quickly and joined the lads from Alpha in their cell sitting room where, as they often did, they brought us drinks as we sat and chatted. Eddie joined us and asked if I could help him obtain his release papers. Before a detainee is released he has to pay a fee (about five pounds) for the processing of his papers. Failure to pay means that release is deferred. Eddie had no money and naturally I was willing to help. However, I'd made it a firm policy not to hand over cash to the inmates, and so arranged to meet him at the jail the following Monday, his expected release date.

I was almost as thrilled as Eddie himself at the decision and it was with great excitement that I set off for Camp Maquinaya on Monday morning, taking my camera so as to capture the very moment of his first steps to freedom. I hadn't anticipated any difficulty over the formalities, but as we waited with growing impatience for the papers to be produced the minutes turned into hours. I began to worry about my preparation for our Bible study at Subic Jail that evening, so when Eddie suggested that if I would leave the money with him, he would call round later to bring me a receipt, I reluctantly agreed. It wasn't just the money; I didn't want to miss seeing him pass from one side of the barbed wire to the other. I returned home full of disappointment.

Shortly before 4 o'clock, I heard my name called out and saw Eddie's face peering through the mosquito screen on the front door. I invited him in and offered him a snack, but he was far too excited to eat or drink. Proudly he presented me with his papers and then for the first time began to tell me the full story of his crime. I'd never pressed for details before.

Eddie had worked as a house-boy/yard-boy, doing work around the house and cleaning his employer's car. Like many others similarly employed, he'd been treated with harshness and contempt. 'He treated me as if I were an animal,' was Eddie's description. One day his employer had pushed him too far and Eddie's temper snapped. Never dreaming that his impulsive action would be fatal, he picked up a bottle and hurled it at his employer. The bottle found its mark and the man was killed. Eddie was charged with murder and his best hope had been that a plea of manslaughter would be accepted. Either way, he had expected a long sentence.

I shared his amazement at his acquittal, for which I could see no grounds in the story he had told me. I believed Eddie had not intended to kill, but he had confessed to causing his employer's death. Eddie explained that his acquittal was due to the fact that the dead man's family had dropped all charges against him. This puzzled me even more, but I didn't want to knock the bloom off Eddie's joy by interrogating him. I tried to keep my manner easy and relaxed, yet underneath in my mind flowed an uneasy stream of questions.

Why would any family drop charges like this? Why would they not want justice meted out to the man who had killed their father, husband, brother or son? As a missionary – and a missionary to prisoners at that – I was called by God to reach out and help criminals, but in a similar situation I would none the less want to see justice done. I would endeavour to love the killer with the love of Christ, to forgive him and long for his repentance, but there are laws which Jesus himself respected. The thief who hung on the cross beside Jesus received forgiveness and the promise of entry into paradise, but Jesus didn't save him from the punishment he'd incurred by breaking the law.

I stilled my doubts as best I could. Maybe the family had been motivated by the fact that Eddie had been severely provoked. The important thing now was to make sure he made good use of his freedom and for this I had to maintain contact with him.

Our church in Olongapo was holding a Christmas party that evening, so before he left I invited Eddie to join us. I wasn't sure he would want to spend his first night of freedom at a church party where he knew so few people, but to my surprise he accepted with alacrity. My anxiety not to lose touch was not based on any doubts as to the reality of his profession of faith nor the sincerity of his good intentions, but I'd learned through Mum's work with juvenile offenders that there are those who, having become Christians, wander away from God when they return to normal life.

As I made my way to the party after the Bible study I was half-prepared for the possibility that he might have changed his mind. Imagine my delight when, as soon as I arrived, I saw that not only was Eddie already there, but he'd also brought a friend. I recognised the friend; it was Jake, one of the pleasantest of the prison officers at Camp Maquinaya. He came from the same *barangay* as Eddie, though I hadn't realised they were friends. Jake couldn't stay long – he was on duty that night and he felt somewhat conspicuous because of the gun he was carrying. He certainly looked like a fish out of water among all the innocent-looking young people.

While poor Jake did his best to efface himself, Eddie threw himself into the fun with enthusiasm and settled in as if he belonged there, joining in all the games and enjoying himself immensely. If the church members were apprehensive on account of his past record, they hid it well. I relaxed a little. Eddie was going to be OK.

Before the party ended I went to say goodbye to him; I had to leave early as I was setting off first thing on Tuesday morning for Manila, where I had to make some official enquiries concerning my prison ministry. I'd be staying the night with some friends of Dorothy and Linda, members of a church founded by David Nellist. Eddie wanted to accompany me on my trip, but I assured him I would be fine. In that case, he said, as he was enjoying the party so much he'd stay to the end and escort Dorothy, Linda and Redemia home. He hoped to call and see us sometime during the week, but couldn't fix a time because he'd be looking for a job in Olongapo. However, we could count on his being at Camp Maquinaya for the service on Friday, as he was looking forward to the youth group's

Christmas presentation. I thought it would have been natural if he'd never wanted to set foot in the jail again, and was encouraged by this indication of his determination to go on with the Lord.

I completed my business in Manila on Tuesday and as soon as I returned on Wednesday I checked with the other girls whether Eddie had called. He hadn't, but then he had warned us he would be job hunting, so I didn't feel too let down.

Thursday came, and still no sign of him. At every knock on the door, Redemia and I leaped up, hoping it was him, but he didn't come. We consoled ourselves with the thought of seeing him the following day.

At last it was Friday the 23rd, the day of our Christmas programme. The tins of biscuits were wrapped, the programme sheets were all prepared for the young people and everything was in place. The four of us set out in the jeepney, accompanied on this occasion by Steve Dulwich, an English minister, and his wife, who were friends of David, working in the Philippines for a few months.

As soon as we arrived at Camp Maquinaya, I was greeted by a young woman, the wife of one of the prison officers: 'Hi, Chrissy. Merry Christmas. Have you heard what happened to Eddie Lazaro?'

'Yes, he was released on Monday.'

'You don't know? He was shot and killed on Tuesday.'

This couldn't possibly be true. Why would anyone shoot Eddie? I felt hollow with shock. The woman was still talking, telling us that according to the story that was circulating, Eddie had been in a restaurant on the main street of Olongapo leading to the naval base (the area where he'd planned to look for a job) and had stolen a watch from an American customer. The police were summoned, Eddie resisted arrest and was shot.

I was quite certain that Eddie would never have done such a thing. No one would be foolish enough to attempt theft in so public a place so soon after being released from jail – much less someone like Eddie, who was determined to put his life right and go on with Christ. Only the night before, at the party, he'd asked the pastor if he would be willing to give him some private Bible instruction, as he had so much to learn. Eddie hadn't committed the crime he was accused of, I was sure of it. And yet he was dead.

I felt ready to sink under a welter of confused emotion. I wanted to scream and cry out to the Lord. But all of this had to be held in check. I had responsibilities to the inmates who were looking forward to the service, and to the young people who had worked so hard to prepare it. No one else appeared to be as devastated as I was; there was some shock and a little distress, but not the turmoil I was experiencing. Only Steve Dulwich seemed to realise what I was going through and put his arm gently on my shoulder.

Inside the compound, we discovered that the young people hadn't yet arrived, which afforded me a brief respite – a few minutes on my own to pray and lay my troubles before the Lord. Alone outside the camp, I struggled to come to terms with what I was feeling. Mixed with my grief at the death of a close friend was a suspicion which was quickly hardening into certainty. During the past few months of working in the jails, I'd often heard the inmates mention 'salvage' (the word is the same in Tagalog and English: an example of Taglish). At first I hadn't understood the term; the contexts in which it was used didn't fit the usual meaning of the word. I later learned that in the Philippines 'salvage' has quite the opposite meaning to saving or rescuing: it is used to refer to the unlawful execution of criminals by the police or others in authority. I became convinced that Eddie was a salvage victim.

As I saw it, this would explain why the family of Eddie's employer had dropped the charges against him. Had he been convicted and given a life sentence this would not have satisfied their desire for revenge. They wanted him to pay with his life, a result they could ensure by dropping the charges and colluding with the police to have him shot on his release. (At the time of Eddie's death, such corruption among the police and the military was commonplace. Since then, power has changed hands twice and the present government is working hard to remedy these abuses.)

I felt full of bitterness towards the police. It was like a physical pain in the pit of my stomach. At the same time, I was conscious of the Holy Spirit reminding me that bitterness is not of God and must be cast out and replaced by love. My human nature tried to justify my anger and rebelled against the conviction of the Spirit. But the word of God requires us unequivocally to love our enemies and I knew I could not allow sin to reign in me. I began to pray in the spirit, speaking in tongues, as I asked the Lord to help me.

As I prayed the pain in my stomach faded away and I knew the victory was mine. Sorrow remained, sorrow for the loss of Eddie, but now I was able to receive the comfort of the Holy Spirit. Most importantly I was free of bitterness, which is so destructive, and ready to take part in the service. I could face the police without hypocrisy. Just then a jeepney drew up, bringing the youth group. I thanked the Lord for his perfect timing.

The inmates gathered for the service were somewhat subdued by the news of Eddie's death, but, as I'd anticipated, it was obviously an encouragement to them to see so many young people willing to come into the jail to bring the Christmas message to them. I was proud of the way the youth group played their part, especially as they had much more to contend with than they'd expected. The police had never guarded our services before, but this time a row of officers, and even the warden himself, stood over us with folded arms and grim faces. They knew I'd been a close friend of Eddie and seemed to suspect that I was unhappy about the circumstances surrounding his death. It was clearly their intention to intimidate me. I did feel a little afraid, but I hung on to the victory I'd won in prayer as I stood up to close the service with the song 'Oh, how he loves you and me'. While I was singing, my eyes met the warden's. At that moment, the Lord gave me his love so that I in turn could look at that man not with hatred but with love. Either embarrassed or ashamed, the warden looked away.

Afterwards, Eddie's friend Jake offered to take Steve Dulwich and me to Eddie's home nearby, where his body was laid out. I wasn't really prepared for what we found there. It was the first time I'd ever seen a dead body and it didn't look like Eddie at all. I wished I hadn't seen him that way. There were no wounds visible so I asked Grace, Eddie's mother, where he had been shot.

'He was shot four times in the back and neck,' she replied.

This added further confirmation to my suspicions.

I'd never met Eddie's family before. There was Grace, his sister and his son Carlito, who was just three years old. Carlito's mother had abandoned him as a baby and Grace had brought him up as her own. The house was full of visitors, so we couldn't talk much, but I visited Grace again and we talked a little about what had happened. She seemed very reluctant to discuss the events surrounding Eddie's death and I suspected there was more to this than simply the pain of bereavement.

'Why don't you try to find out the truth of what happened?' I asked.

'Chrissy,' she replied, 'I still have my daughter and Carlito. If I take any risks, I might lose them too.'

I wasn't the only one to feel intimidated by the police.

Several days later, the newspaper carried a story purporting to give the details of Eddie's death, and the alleged circumstances were entirely different from those in the first account I'd been given. This time, Eddie was supposed to have stolen money from the restaurant cash register and stabbed the police officer who was trying to arrest him. As he fell badly wounded to the ground, the officer managed to shoot Eddie. I found it impossible to believe that a man in that condition could have placed four bullets so neatly and accurately in Eddie's back.

For many weeks afterwards, officers would stand guard at our services in Camp Maquinaya and in order to safeguard our ministry we affected to be unaware of the reason for their presence. The Lord continued to give us love for them, and indeed we recognised that their need of Christ was as great as that of the inmates.

Grace never was able to search for the truth. For myself, I would have been willing to risk taking the matter further, but I couldn't jeopardise her safety or that of the children. So I managed to avoid a clash with officialdom over Eddie; but it was a different story with Danny.

7

Danny

Gunshots rang out through the night. They sounded quite close, though I couldn't be sure. No one else seemed concerned, so perhaps it was just firecrackers after all. They could sound remarkably like gunfire. Anyway, we were right next door to the jail and the police station in the Municipal Hall, so we'd be safe enough.

Redemia and I were leading a Bible study in the home of Simon, one of our neighbours in the compound. The idea of beginning a Bible study had come from Simon's cousin-in-law Francisco, who had simply knocked on our door one day and asked us to start a study group for him and several others. He rounded up a number of young men and women, his friends and neighbours, and we'd been meeting with them regularly. Francisco had become a Christian and the level of interest among the others was high.

The following day I discovered that the feeling of security I'd derived from being close to the Municipal Hall had been completely unfounded: the shooting had happened in Subic Jail itself. One of the inmates, a boy called Danny, had been shot in the face by a police officer. I'd been in the Philippines for eight months now, long enough not to be easily shocked by such an incident, especially after Eddie's death, but still it was horrifying to think of it happening to someone we knew.

Danny had been in Subic Jail ever since we first began to visit. He was charged with assaulting a policeman, but his case had not yet come to court. He wasn't a troublesome prisoner; rather the reverse. For some time he'd been a trusty (a well-behaved prisoner granted special privileges), which meant he was allowed to work outside the jail in other areas of the Municipal Hall and often ran errands for the officers. This made it all the more surprising that he'd been shot; it was unlikely he'd been trying to escape.

My surprise receded somewhat when I learned that the officer responsible was Patrolman Apin, and that he'd been drunk on duty at the time. Living so close to the jail and visiting often, I'd gained a fair amount of knowledge about the various officers and their characters, and I knew Patrolman Apin had treated inmates harshly before, including Danny. In his drunken state, Apin had pointed his gun at Danny's head as a joke – and then pulled the trigger. Danny's quick reflexes had saved him from instant death, but he was very badly wounded.

Redemia was the first to visit him at the General Hospital in Olongapo and she returned so distressed by what she'd seen that I decided to visit him myself. I felt strongly that I should lay hands on him and pray for his healing. This was my first visit to a General Hospital in the Philippines, and it gave me a real taste of culture shock.

As I walked along the corridors I could hardly believe the evidence of my senses. I remembered the almost aggressive cleanliness of British hospitals, where the smell of disinfectant clings to your clothes for hours after a short visit. The smell here was utterly nauseating. As I glanced into the various wards as I passed, it was like being taken back in time and witnessing the scenes pictured in my school history books about the Crimean War. Chaotic disorder prevailed everywhere, as if the hospital had been overwhelmed by a major disaster. There had been no disaster; this was just the normal state of affairs.

In Britain, there are nurses constantly checking on their patients, but here there were none. Instead, each bed was surrounded by the patient's family and friends on whom devolved the task of comforting, feeding and caring for their sick relative. The heat was almost unendurable even for a healthy person and there were no fans except those provided by the patients themselves. There was a general air of dilapidation; the walls obviously hadn't seen a paintbrush in a long time.

When at last I found Danny lying alone and motionless with no one taking the slightest notice of him, I barely recognised him. His face and neck were swollen to twice their normal size; the bullet had grazed his face as he leaped out of the way, damaging his eye, nose and mouth. None of the staff, when I eventually found them, could tell me whether the damage to his eye was serious, nor whether it would require surgery. Danny had so far received provisional first aid, nothing more. His face was a mass of stitches and was covered with flies. He was still wearing the clothes in which he'd arrived two days ago and since then no one had washed him. His hands and clothes were crusted with dried blood, as was the single sheet on which he was lying. The sheet was rumpled and beneath it I could see the filthy stains on the mattress. I felt like being sick.

Danny was in such pain that he was barely aware of my presence, but as I gazed at his injuries I became convinced that God was going to perform a miracle for him. I laid hands on him and prayed that the Lord would reach down and touch him, and grant him complete healing.

After this first visit, I felt such concern for Danny that I began to visit him daily. Francisco offered to come with me to act as interpreter, as Danny knew no English and I wasn't yet proficient in Tagalog. We brought an electric fan which, though it didn't have much effect on the heat, at least helped to keep the flies away. We also provided clean sheets and a set of Francisco's clothes for Danny to wear while we took his own away to wash them.

At first Danny was unable to speak, but I was buoyed up by my inner conviction that God was going to heal him. And within a few days we began to see an answer to our prayers as the horrific injuries started to heal and Danny's speech was restored. There still wasn't much medical care, but at least he'd been put on a dextrose drip, which was something. Yet God was doing a greater work in Danny than his physical healing.

Through Francisco, I talked to him about God's love, explaining from Scripture how the Lord Jesus Christ had died in his place. It was wonderful to see how, in such a desperate situation, the grace of God evoked a response in Danny's heart, bringing him to the point where, as we led him in a short prayer, he acknowledged his need of a Saviour and surrendered his life to Christ.

One day I arrived at the hospital alone to find Danny's bed empty. My mind full of awful possibilities, I looked around for someone who could tell me what had happened, but of course there were no nursing staff to be seen. As the minutes passed my anxiety mounted and I decided to take a chance that the elderly man in the opposite bed would understand English. Thankfully he did, and was able to reassure me that Danny was fine and had just gone to get himself something to eat. He was a very friendly man and amazingly cheerful in spite of his circumstances. He was waiting to have his leg amputated and his wife was in the next bed suffering from a stomach complaint. It was hard to believe that this man was about to lose his leg in consequence of a simple scratch on his toe. Because of the lack of clean water and poor hygiene, and because he could not afford antiseptics, this small scratch had led to gangrene in the foot, with the result that several of his toes were now missing and what remained of the foot was black with decay.

As I looked at this poor elderly couple who had no

visitors to care for them I reflected on the way in which we in England so easily take for granted the health care provision which is available to us, and how quick we are to grumble about cuts in welfare benefits. We complain about the rising cost of prescriptions, yet a Filipino has to pay a day's wage just to consult the doctor, before he even obtains a prescription. If he is admitted to hospital, he knows he won't be allowed to leave until he has paid his bill. If he can't pay, he has to stay, incurring more debt the longer he remains there. A first-hand experience of third-world poverty in a country which doesn't enjoy the advantage of a National Health Service, and where children die of measles, diarrhoea and malnutrition, certainly makes one appreciate the blessings of living in the western world. No government service is ever perfect, but we do have so much to thank God for.

As if to confirm the contrast, Danny returned with the boiled eggs he had bought from a canteen, having had to carry his bottle of dextrose with him out of the hospital.

It was never my intention to get involved in the politics of Danny's case – I was simply a missionary offering pastoral care and moral support. But circumstances forced my hand.

One day when Francisco and I arrived, Danny already had a visitor, a woman. This was unusual, as apart from us Danny seemed never to have visitors. Not wanting to intrude, we withdrew until the woman had left.

When we returned, Danny immediately launched into an animated explanation. I couldn't understand a word of his rapid Tagalog, but Francisco told me that Danny's visitor was the wife of Patrolman Apin. She had offered to pay for Danny to have plastic surgery on his face and to arrange for him to be released from jail and go to live somewhere in the country. In return, she wanted him to promise not to press charges against her husband.

Although Danny was twenty-one, he was very naive and had taken Mrs Apin's offer at face value, believing implicitly all she told him. However, knowing that very few Filipinos could afford to pay for plastic surgery, and remembering what had happened to Eddie, I was instantly convinced that Danny was being set up. I'd heard stories of other people being taken away to the country – and the arrangement wasn't made out of concern for their welfare but in order to conceal their whereabouts so that they would not be missed if they disappeared suddenly.

It was up to me to do something because Danny had no one else to take an interest in him. I went to see his mother, but she refused to 'waste' her money on the jeepney ride to the hospital. The choice I faced wasn't much of a choice at all: either sit around, do nothing and risk a repeat of Eddie's fate; or put my own safety in jeopardy and fight for justice for Danny. I simply couldn't leave him at the mercy of the police officer who'd shot him, so I began to pray for the Lord's guidance and wisdom, to lead both Danny and me to safety.

What my commitment to help Danny was going to mean in practice, I didn't precisely know; and in the event the need for action arose before I'd had time to seek advice. By now, Patrolman Apin had learned of my daily visits to the hospital and perhaps it was because he was afraid I would interfere with his plans that his wife went to see Danny and told him he'd be leaving that same day. I had no plans of my own ready, so I did the only thing I could think of: I went straight to the hospital director and pleaded with him not to allow Danny to be discharged. 'We need the bed,' he said coldly, and that was that.

Patrolman Apin arrived with his wife in a rented jeepney and poor Danny, suspecting nothing, went without protest. I followed them to the jeepney, wanting to demonstrate that I intended to concern myself with Danny's welfare. As the jeepney pulled away, Danny waved and smiled, such an innocent, trusting smile. I forced myself to smile back, but inwardly I was shaking with fear. I was only twenty-one myself and very inexperienced. Less than a year ago I hadn't even had to worry about paying an electricity bill, and now a man's life might depend on my doing the right thing. But 'God has not given us a spirit of fear, but of power and of love and of a sound mind' (2 Tim 1:7). With this assurance, I rebuked my fear and at once experienced the truth of Christ's promise: 'I am with you always, even to the end of the age' (Mt 28:20).

As quickly as I could, I made my way back to Subic and went immediately to the jail to ask where Danny had been taken. The police were very offhand with me, even contemptuous, though in the past we'd been on the friendliest terms. Danny, they told me, was back in their custody and I was not permitted to speak to him.

I tried again the following day, taking Francisco with me, and this time I was successful. Danny showed me a paper he'd been told to sign. It was an affidavit of desistance; that is, a statement affirming that he did not wish to press charges against Apin. The police had exerted a lot of pressure and repeated all Mrs Apin's promises, and Danny had signed. Gently I tried to make him understand that Patrolman Apin couldn't possibly afford to fulfil these promises and that once he was freed from the threat of prosecution, Danny himself would be in grave danger. I promised that if he wanted to change his mind, I would do all I could to support him.

Danny was pathetically surprised that anyone should be taking an interest in him. He had known so little love in his life and couldn't understand why I, whom he'd known for so short a time, should try to help him when even his mother showed no concern on his behalf. It was the love of Jesus in my heart, I told him, that caused me to care about him.

He thought about my offer for a while. It didn't come naturally to him to suspect people of ulterior motives, but once he'd grasped what lay in store for him – and perhaps for others too, if Apin went unpunished – he decided to ask for the affidavit to be revoked.

My role in persuading him placed me in open conflict with the police, which on the face of it looked like a very unequal contest, especially since, from then on, I was more or less on my own. Only Francisco remained willing to be actively involved and many people, convinced that I was taking too big a risk, tried to dissuade me from pursuing Danny's case. I wasn't sure how far I was risking my personal safety, or my prison ministry, but I did know I couldn't abandon Danny.

The day of reckoning was not long in coming. Early one morning we answered a knock at the door to find one of the Subic policemen bringing a message from his superior officer, Lieutenant Santos: would I please go and see the lieutenant in his office? There was no question of disobeying the summons, so I set off for the Municipal Hall.

When I entered the lieutenant's office, the first thing I saw was Mrs Apin sitting at the far end of the room. Lieutenant Santos began to speak. In the past he'd always been supportive of our ministry, but there was no mistaking the fact that his present purpose was to warn me off. His voice was quiet and his manner sympathetic, but the message was plain: for the sake of my own safety, I should take his advice and drop the matter. I wasn't sure exactly what he was implying, but I replied as firmly as I could that I would help Danny for as long as he wanted me to.

Mrs Apin, who had been simmering with barely suppressed anger during this exchange, could contain herself no longer and erupted with a stream of filthy abuse which even Lieutenant Santos, who was obviously embarrassed, couldn't stem. She was consumed with rage and bitterness against me, accusing me of the most unspeakable things. The tirade ended with her screaming that I was trying to destroy her husband. Though it was disturbing to find myself the target of her virulence, I didn't actually feel any anger towards her. I could understand that she was afraid for her husband. As calmly as I could, I replied, 'No, Mrs Apin. I understand that you are standing up for your husband, but I have no personal grudge against him. He's fortunate to have someone who cares for him. Danny has no one except me and all I want is to stand by him and see that he receives justice.'

A protracted silence followed. Eventually, Lieutenant Santos said that the judge who had witnessed the signing of the affidavit was waiting to see me in his office on the next floor.

The judge's hostility was less ambiguous than Lieutenant Santos'. In no uncertain terms he told me I had no business to meddle in the affair and that it would be greatly to my advantage to keep out of what didn't concern me. 'The weapon of a missionary is the Bible,' he said, 'and you should stick to that, because the weapons of the police are guns.' Incongruously he added, 'I'm not trying to scare you.'

I made no reply and, rightly taking my silence as a refusal to comply, he began to threaten me more openly. 'I could make it impossible for you to remain in the Philippines as a missionary, and then what would you do?'

'Well, sir, I think I'd go to Africa.' I wasn't trying to be cheeky. I just meant that if I was prevented from preaching the gospel in the Philippines, then I was sure God would open other doors.

With that, the interview was over, but I'd left the judge in no doubt that I wasn't to be intimidated into abandoning Danny. My greatest fear was that I wouldn't have time to see things through to a conclusion before my ten months came to an end. My return flight was just a short time ahead and I knew only too well how protracted judicial processes could be. It had in fact become clear to me recently that I wouldn't be leaving the Philippines for good and that God had much more for me to do here. I was ready for a break, but that was all it would be. However, I was worried about leaving Danny at this crucial stage.

Thankfully, Francisco was now as committed as I was and assured me he would take care of everything. Nothing was settled before I left and I was dependent on Francisco for news. While I was in England, things moved very fast (which didn't often happen in the Philippines) and Francisco, true to his word, wrote to tell me the outcome, which was mostly good. For while no charges were being pressed against Patrolman Apin, Danny had been acquitted of the assault charge on which he'd been detained and after his release had found work in Manila, where he would be safe.

I was profoundly relieved that Danny's story had ended so differently from Eddie's. But it wasn't until months later, after I'd returned to the Philippines, that I received confirmation of just how real the threat had been.

It took a while for the Subic police to overcome their hostility, but in the end I regained their friendship and even an extra degree of respect. Patrolman Apin, however, never forgave me. Then one day, on a regular visit to Camp Maquinaya, when I'd been back eight months, I was stunned to discover that Apin was being detained as an inmate. Late one night, in a quiet spot not far from Subic Town, he had forced a nineteen-year-old boy to strip himself naked and ordered him to run. As the terrified boy fled, Apin shot him in the back.

My blood ran cold when I heard this story. It could so easily have been Danny. My involvement in his case brought me a great deal of trouble and anxiety, but I thank the Lord that I did it.

8

The Vision

I flew back to England in the summer of 1984 both physically and emotionally drained, feeling that the past ten months had provided enough harrowing experiences to last a lifetime. Yet I had a vision in my heart of what the Lord wanted to accomplish through me when I returned to the Philippines.

I saw clearly now that my work so far was only a beginning. Taking the gospel to the inmates in the jails was one thing, but what prospect was there for them when they were eventually released? All they had to look forward to was unemployment, poverty and discrimination. Take Rhey, for example. Rhey, the mayor of Alpha block at Camp Maquinaya, had killed a man with a pair of scissors and though there was no doubt that he had acted in self-defence it was more than unexpected – it was a miracle – that when his case was heard, he was released.

Nothing in his previous experience had fitted him for anything other than a life of crime. Orphaned as a young child and thrown out onto the streets by his stepmother when he was only seven, he had turned to selling drugs in order to survive. It was the only life he knew. He'd been attracted to Olongapo by the possibility which the naval base afforded of earning dollars, and had worked with a

member of the US military who imported the drugs which
Rhey, with his many contacts, was able to sell for high
prices. He made a lot of money and was a well-known
figure in the bars around the base, and though the police
were aware of his operations he was always able to buy
himself out of trouble until he was arrested and charged
with murder.

On his release, Rhey faced an impossible situation. Having had no education, he could neither read nor write and
so could not even fill in an application for a job, which in
any case he'd be unlikely to get, given his record. Drug
dealing was the only way he knew of making money, but as
a newly converted Christian this avenue was obviously
closed to him. How was he to support himself and his
family?

When I visited him after he came out of jail, I found him
and Ning, his wife, squatting in an empty derelict house
entirely bare of furniture and with gaping holes in the roof
through which the rain poured relentlessly. They had a few
cooking pans but no food; they were using the pans to
catch the rain. To add to their problems, six-year-old
Precy, the elder of their two daughters, suffered from a
congenital condition which rendered her unable to walk,
talk or eat solid food. She never communicated with her
parents at all and they believed she was also mentally handicapped, though because of her physical problems it was
difficult to be sure.

I had spent the whole of those first ten months preaching, teaching and caring for the spiritual needs of those I
met in the jails, but now the Lord was showing me that the
gospel is more than 'pie in the sky'. Jesus was concerned
not only with their eternal well being but also with their
physical welfare here and now. It was not enough to have
preached the gospel to people like Rhey – they needed help
to become established in their new life with Christ once
they faced the harsh reality which awaited them on the
other side of the barbed wire. Thus was planted the seed

of my vision of a rehabilitation home for ex-prisoners, their wives and their families.

Equally urgent were the needs of the children in the Subic area. Under Linda's leadership, the four of us had extended our children's outreach work to many of the surrounding villages, but so far we had dealt only with spiritual and emotional needs. I now envisaged, in addition to the rehabilitation home, a children's refuge home to cater for two different classes of children.

First, there were the many youngsters who were deprived of education because their parents couldn't afford to send them to school. Elementary education was really quite cheap, but parents often failed to enrol their children if they couldn't afford to buy them decent clothes or if they needed them at home to take care of younger brothers and sisters while they tried to find work. Some of the poorest, who couldn't even feed their children properly, saw no point in encouraging them to study on an empty stomach. Kids like these would remain trapped in poverty all their lives. Short of a miracle, the only way out lay in education.

The other group were the children of inmates in Camp Maquinaya. Unbelievable as it sounds, some of these children actually lived with their parents inside the jail, where they regularly witnessed drunken brawls, drug abuse, prostitution and homosexuality. To have a child growing up in this environment, which the inmates themselves called 'this dark place', was a situation no parent would willingly countenance, but these parents had no choice. For them it was the only alternative to allowing their children to starve alone on the streets. God had given me a burning desire to reach out to them and provide them with a home where they would receive love, stability and an education. Above all, I was mindful of his word: 'Train up a child in the way he should go, and when he is old he will not depart from it' (Prov 22:6).

The final strand of my vision related to the particular

difficulties which newly released prisoners found in becoming part of a worshipping community. Shortly after his release, Rhey went with us to church. With his scruffy clothes and unkempt hair he looked very out of place. I felt uncomfortable at the way people stood aloof from him, though in truth Rhey's rough exterior, his body covered in tattoos and his scarred face presented an alarming appearance to anyone who didn't know him. People like Rhey needed a spiritual home where they could feel accepted, and I believed God was calling me to create a place where they could worship freely. I was concerned also about our neighbours in Subic Town who needed Christ and for whom there was no nearby church where the gospel was preached.

This was the vision I carried home. A rehabilitation home; a children's refuge; a place of worship: a work which would be called the Philippine Outreach Centre.

During my three months in England a number of churches invited me to speak about my work and I took the opportunity to share my vision for the future. After many of these visits I came away very encouraged by the enthusiastic response of the many people who wanted to be kept informed about the Philippine Outreach Centre.

It was in England that I had my first serious encounter with culture shock. Apart from the General Hospital at Olongapo, I'd absorbed the impact of my environment in the Philippines without much trouble, adjusting quite easily to the lower standard of living and to sharing my home with insects and other forms of wildlife. But when I walked around Manchester and saw people who had spent more on the clothes they wore than many Filipinos have invested in their homes, I was struck by a deep sense of the unfairness of things. As I wandered round the huge, spotless supermarkets I recalled shopping trips in Olongapo, where I'd seen mice, and even rats, scurrying along the floors of the grocery stores. 'Excuse me,' I'd said to one store owner, 'but you have a rat on your bags of sugar.'

'Oh, yes,' she'd replied, 'we have a lot of those.'

In the meat section of the supermarket, I remembered my first visit to a Philippine meat market: row upon row of stalls where the meat hung sweating through the heat of the day. The vendors waged a continual but hopeless war against the flies which buzzed around in clouds. Add to this the fact that the most popular meat was pork, and you've got a paradise for bacteria. It was a world away from the hygienic refrigerated packages in front of me. And the prices! In the Philippines our weekly budget for rice, fish and vegetables was only 100 pesos (the rate of exchange then was 18 pesos to the pound) and pork and chicken were luxuries.

The comfort – the opulence, even, as it now appeared – of my own home and those of my friends made me uneasy, and once, when I was taken for a meal at an expensive restaurant, I was so upset by the prices that my friend and I had to leave and find somewhere with a more modest menu. Culture shock was in danger of turning into resentment of all this western affluence, until God began to show me that it is not necessarily wrong for Christians to have money; in fact, my own work had benefited from the generosity of his people. And just as I shouldn't condemn Filipinos for their poverty, neither should I condemn the British for their prosperity. Like St Paul, I had to learn to live both with humble means and with plenty (Phil 4:12). None the less, my return in September to the little house in Subic felt like a return to normality.

When my plane landed in Manila, I was welcomed not only by Dorothy, Linda and Redemia but also, to my delight, by many of the young people who met for Bible study in Simon's house. It was good to be reunited with the other three girls, but I wasn't actually going to be living with them for much longer.

David Nellist had been very enthusiastic about my vision for the Philippine Outreach Centre and encouraged me to go forward with it, but at the same time, his own long-term vision was still to train Filipinos to evangelise their own nation. We therefore agreed together that my work and his should become separate, developing on independent lines with mutual love and respect. I would never forget how the Lord used David to call me to the Philippines, nor how he helped me take my first steps as a missionary.

Though I felt sure the decision to pursue separate ministries was the right one, it meant I had to pioneer the Philippine Outreach Centre alone. When I first conceived my vision, I'd thought in terms of continuing under the umbrella of David's mission, but I now began to pray and seek God's will as to the way forward on my own. I rented a small bungalow not too far away and prepared to move in. I'd be on my own, but only for two weeks because Mum was coming out to visit me and spend Christmas in the Philippines.

Just two weeks. That was all Satan needed to draw me into a situation which laid waste all my hopes. Ironically, the trouble had its roots in the Bible study group at Simon's house, which Redemia and I had resumed on my return.

Simon lived alone, as his wife was in America at the time. This sort of arrangement is not uncommon in the Philippines; it's the ambition of many Filipinos to reach America in search of a better way of life, and if one partner in a marriage succeeds in obtaining a visa, he or she will emigrate alone in the hope that the other will be able to follow later. Simon, however, was finding it difficult to cope with his loneliness and began to get very depressed. His wife's cousin, Edwin (who was also a member of the Bible study group) used to visit him often, but all his attempts to shake Simon out of his depression failed. Simon lost interest in everything, became increasingly lethargic and didn't even bother to eat.

While I was still living with Dorothy, Linda and Redemia, we began inviting him round for meals from time to time. He'd become a friend, and we were concerned at the state he was in. Then, when I moved into the bungalow, Simon started to visit me there, bringing questions about the Bible study and asking my advice about spiritual things.

I was still only twenty-two and very naive. I was also ignorant of many aspects of Filipino culture and was unaware that to a Filipino, a single woman who opened her door to him was also opening her heart. It took a while for me to realise that Simon's feelings for me were much more than those of a friend, but when I did, I was horrified and made it clear that the sort of relationship he wanted was not an option. But Simon, though a very gentle man, was also very persistent; and I, on my own for the first time in my life, was very vulnerable. Simon took advantage of my vulnerability and before I knew it, I was emotionally involved with him. It never went further than that, but I knew it was wrong and I knew I had to end it, yet I lacked the will to act. Guilt and remorse tormented me, but I was unable truly to repent and confess my fault. The struggle was sharp but mercifully brief and when I finally turned to the Lord in repentance his grace and forgiveness were instantaneous.

On the day my mother arrived, Dorothy came to pay a farewell visit. Her time with David's mission was over and she was leaving the next day. As we were talking, Edwin called and asked to speak to me outside. As soon as we were alone, he dropped his bombshell: he'd found out about my involvement with Simon and intended to make his knowledge public unless I agreed to marry him. Still reeling under the shock of discovery, it never occurred to me that he thought things had gone much further between Simon and me than was actually the case. I felt so guilty anyway that I never thought to go into details with him. Pulling myself together, I told Edwin that I couldn't possibly marry him, whereupon he threatened to tell his cousin

(Simon's wife) about me and assured me that his family would take revenge on me. Somehow I managed to get rid of him and the rest of the day passed in a blur.

The following day Edwin returned. He had obviously been taking drugs, something I'd never known him do before, and, in front of my mother, repeated his threats and his demand that I marry him. Of course, Mum told him it was out of the question, so after raging and shouting at us Edwin went home and phoned his cousin in America.

Poor Mum. I'd done it to her again. She was still suffering from jet lag and culture shock, and here she was facing the situation all mothers dread. She'd assumed from Edwin's account that I'd had a sexual relationship with Simon and of course she was devastated. Not realising her mistake, I naturally didn't disabuse her. Her anger and disappointment seemed perfectly justified by what I had done and it was quite some time before the truth came out.

Despite her anger, Mum's chief concern was for my safety. We were both worried by Edwin's threats of revenge, which we soon discovered were not idle. On several consecutive nights, as we lay in bed, we heard footsteps and furtive whispers outside our window. The sense of being spied on was terrifying. A few days later, we returned from shopping to find crosses painted in blood all over the walls of the house and the initial 'C' scrawled in blood at the doorway. We couldn't doubt that Edwin was responsible, though we never saw him, until, on Christmas Day, I had an accidental meeting with him and his sister in the street. As soon as he saw me, he sprang at me, punched me in the face and began beating me up until his sister dragged him off. I staggered home wondering how much more I could take.

One of the worst aspects of this nightmare was that we felt unable to ask anyone for help. Dorothy had gone, and to involve Linda would only make her afraid too. We were too ashamed to tell the people at church. Occasionally we took refuge with Phil and Audrey Houghton, an American missionary couple who ran the Military Mission for US servicemen in Subic. They had become good friends to me and though we didn't confide in them, it was a relief just to have fellowship in an atmosphere of peace and sanity.

We no longer felt safe in our own home. Mum had never liked the house anyway (it was very bug-ridden), so we decided to move. We found a bungalow in another *barangay* of Subic called Pamatawan which, being on the outskirts of the town, put both physical and psychological distance between us and our problems.

Throughout this trial, Mum and I struggled to keep the prison work going with Redemia's help. I avoided going to Subic Jail because it was so near to where Simon and Edwin lived, but in addition to Camp Maquinaya I was by now making weekly visits to Iba Jail at the request of a local pastor. Iba lay a one-and-a-half-hour bus ride to the north of Subic. I often wept as I sang and preached to the inmates, knowing that my words about sin and repentance were for me as much as for them. I'd let the Lord down so badly and jeopardised my whole mission. I knew that gossip about me was rife – Edwin had fulfilled his threat there too – and I had foolishly given room for it.

With all the stress I began to lose weight and looked so very pale and ill that finally Mum insisted that I go home for a break and allow her to continue the ministry in my absence. We booked a flight a few weeks after Christmas and I flew home in despair. I hadn't told Mum that I had decided never to return to the Philippines.

9

'My Grace Is Sufficient'

When Dad met me at the airport he didn't recognise me until I spoke to him. He was visibly shocked to see me looking so pale and thin. I'd dreaded facing questions from people at church, but in fact no one asked any. My physical appearance seemed reason enough for my early return. However, I wanted to be honest, so I let it be known, without going into details, that I'd failed the Lord.

I was so sure he'd never be willing to use me again on the mission field that almost as soon as I arrived home I began looking for work. I found a job in a technical drawing office and tried to pick up the threads of my former life. As I sat at my desk, my heart and mind were in the Philippines, but I never spoke to the Lord about it. I'd repented and he had forgiven me, but I would never dare ask for a second chance.

Mum wrote telling me that Remedia had moved in with her and that the two of them had begun attending a small church in Olongapo, called the Born-Again Christians' Den, whose pastor, James, was helping them with the prison ministry. James was an ex-prisoner himself and related easily to the inmates. Mum had also started a new children's outreach in Pamatawan, and, as if all this were not enough, had established an evangelistic work of her

own among Filipina women in the remote rural districts
around Subic. While I rejoiced at what God was doing
through Mum, it made me even more keenly aware of
what I had lost. My own life seemed like a pointless succes-
sion of empty days. I wondered what I would do with the
rest of my life.

The graciousness of God never ceases to amaze me. One
Sunday morning in church, when I'd been home about six
weeks, I had a fresh experience of his love and received
from him the assurance that his power had redeemed all my
failures. He spoke to me in the words of 2 Corinthians
12:9: 'My grace is sufficient for you, for My strength is
made perfect in weakness.' I had an overwhelming sense of
his grace in my heart and I knew he was giving me the
second chance I hadn't dared ask for. Full of thankfulness,
I renewed my vow to serve him in the Philippines.

After that, things moved quickly. A few weeks after
Mum came home in February, I was ready to go back. In
preparation for my return, I meditated on the events of the
past few months, knowing that God works through trials
for our good and that there were lessons for me to learn
from my failure. Painfully, I recognised that I had glibly
assumed that as a missionary I was somehow immune to
the temptations which beset other people. For all the fact
that I was so frequently engaged in preaching about the
seriousness of sin, I never really reckoned with the possibility that I would fall into sin myself. I'd allowed myself to
become spiritually proud and self-righteous, too sure of my
own strength. I believe God permitted me to fall from his
grace for a short time so that I would learn the full extent
of my dependence on him. It is easy to say, 'Without God I
can do nothing;' it is much harder to grasp the reality. I
thanked the Lord for teaching me this so early in my
ministry.

I returned to the little bungalow in Pamatawan in March
1985, chastened and humbled but with a renewed vision

for the work ahead. I didn't expect it to be easy. With my reputation in tatters as a result of the gossip spread by Edwin, I had to be prepared for hostility and mistrust. It might take years to re-establish my credibility before I could even begin to think of setting up the Philippine Outreach Centre.

I was so grateful to Remedia for standing by me. She had decided to join me permanently and together we resumed the familiar pattern of children's outreaches and prison work. We concentrated on Iba Jail and Camp Maquinaya, adding weekly Bible studies to our regular services in both places. This meant making four trips a week to Camp Maquinaya, as for security reasons Alpha and Bravo blocks were never now opened on the same day, and each group had to be visited separately.

It was satisfying to be back where I felt I belonged, doing the work I knew was mine, but how hard it was to react calmly to the cold stares and contempt of those who had believed Edwin's gossip. Phil and Audrey Houghton at the Military Mission were always there for me and their friendship helped me find the courage to go on. Making light of the demands of his own work, Phil made time to come with us to the jails from time to time. He and Audrey treated me like a daughter; to me they were (and still are) 'Mom and Pop Houghton'.

Simon's wife had returned from America and the couple were immediately reconciled. I met her one day in the market and asked if we could talk. It was only then that I discovered that Edwin had told her (and others) that I was pregnant. I explained that this was impossible – that Simon and I had not had a physical relationship. I apologised to her for what had happened and assured her that Simon's feelings for me had only arisen as a result of his missing her so much. Shortly afterwards she and Simon left the Philippines to go to America together.

Not long after this, Edwin took to cycling past our house and I schooled myself to return a polite greeting to the insults he hurled at me. This had its effect and eventually I was able to have a reasonable conversation with him. He admitted that it was he and his friends who had spied on Mum and me and that they had painted the walls of our house with expired human blood which Edwin had taken from the medical lab where he worked on the US naval base. He still insisted he wanted to marry me, but the firmness of my refusal finally convinced him and he accepted it. Later, when he was married to someone else, we were able to meet as friends.

These encounters went some way towards resolving the situation, but what really helped me to put the past behind me was a visit I made to a group of small islands in the southern part of the Philippines. I couldn't have afforded the trip had it not been for the fact that when I flew back in March, a special promotional offer entitled every international passenger on Philippine Airlines to an internal flight at half price. Through a network of mutual acquaintances, I'd received an invitation from a Pastor Thomas on the island of Bohol to visit him and take part in his prison ministry. The cheap ticket appeared to be God's provision, and confirmation of his will that I should go.

From Manila I flew first to the island of Cebu, where I stayed for a few days with some English friends of Linda who ran a children's mission called Sunshine Corner, before flying on to Bohol to spend a fortnight with Pastor Thomas.

I knew that Thomas had founded a church and a Bible school and that he led his students in various forms of evangelism, especially in the jails, but I'd never met him and I wondered, as the small aircraft flew across the Bohol Strait, how I would recognise him when we landed. However, all uncertainty dissolved when I stepped off the plane at Tagbilaran airport (airport? it looked more like an ordinary bus shelter back home) and saw a huge Filipino surrounded by a group of young people carrying a banner emblazoned with the words 'Welcome, Sister Chrissy'.

Thomas placed an enormous garland of exotic flowers round my neck and I felt instantly at home.

Bohol was a tiny island paradise, largely untouched by western influence. There was a hotel for foreign holiday-makers, but its guests can't have ventured far: in my two weeks there, I met only Filipinos. The island had few modern amenities, but everything was so clean. After the dirt, the squalor even, of Subic Bay, I was entranced by the golden beaches, the greenness of the dense vegetation and the purity of the air. The freshness of the scene felt like a new start in itself.

Thomas' house in Tagbilaran, where I stayed, was made of *kawayan* (bamboo) and *nipa* (palm leaves) and was as clean as everything else. I was delighted with it, despite Thomas' tendency to apologise for its lack of modern facilities.

On my first evening (Filipino Christians don't believe in wasting time) I was the speaker at a service in Thomas' church. The Holy Spirit's presence among us was unmistakable and as I saw the many young people in the congregation eagerly responding, being challenged to take part in prison outreach, my own heart overflowed with gratitude to the God who was still willing to use me as his instrument to speak to others.

It was the beginning of a very precious time for me. In the following days, as I visited Tagbilaran's two jails with Pastor Thomas and his young people, I discovered a new joy in serving the Lord and, freed from the problems which dogged me at Subic, I was able to appropriate the full reality of my restoration. The Lord was with me as I sang and preached to the inmates, and I had the privilege of seeing many profess the desire to receive Jesus as their Lord and Saviour.

One incident in particular remains with me, and this concerned not an inmate but a police officer. Unaware that he'd even been listening to what I was saying, I was first startled, then thrilled, when he indicated that he too wished to become a Christian. This was the first time either Thomas or I had been able to lead a policeman to the Lord; they were notoriously harder to reach than even murderers and drug addicts. It seemed like a special pledge that God was with me in my work.

I returned to Subic with my confidence renewed, sure now that if I only trusted him, God would use me in some way, even if the Philippine Outreach Centre lay far in the future. For now, I was glad to be back and visiting Iba and Camp Maquinaya again. I had enjoyed my time on Bohol, but the inmates here were my family and I had missed them.

At Mum's suggestion, I'd joined James's church, where Remedia was already a member. Because it was situated near the main gate of the naval base in Olongapo, the Born-Again Christians' Den was often visited by service people, but the members, who included a lot of young people, were mostly Filipinos, as was James. It was a small fellowship which James himself had started, and the services, which were relaxed and informal, were conducted in Taglish. James's own ministry with the church kept him fairly busy, but he continued to help Remedia and me in the jails, and from time to time some of the young people came along too. It was good to belong to a church that was so supportive of my ministry and I was very happy there. And it was there too that I first met Dondie.

10

Stepping Stone

Good news: Jason was to be released from Iba! When we
first met him, Jason was being detained at Camp Maquinaya because of his drug abuse, and at that time he made it
plain that there was no room for God in his life; but when
he was later transferred to Iba a marked change came over
him. The preaching of the gospel began to penetrate his
indifference and it was not long before he gave his heart to
the Lord.

Jason was only twenty-four, and on his release he went
to live with his mother. Though not rich by any means, the
family was moderately well off compared to those of most
ex-prisoners, so this seemed a hopeful arrangement. James
and I invited him to join us at church on Sundays and he
came faithfully for several weeks, fitting in well with the
others of his age group, who did their best to make him feel
accepted.

One Sunday he appeared distressed. He approached me
and asked me to pray for him. 'I need a place to stay,' he
said. 'The problem with staying at my mother's is that all
my old friends know where I am and keep trying to get me
back onto drugs. Sister Chrissy, I don't want to go back to
that kind of life.'

Twenty years ago a similar plea for help had set my

mother on the path to creating a refuge for young offenders. Now, incredibly, I sensed the Lord reminding me of my own vision of a rehabilitation home. I heard his voice say: 'The time is now.'

'Lord, you can't really mean that!' We were not yet ready for a rehabilitation programme. I'd been so sure that it lay far in the future and felt miserably unprepared and inadequate. Then I remembered: 'My grace is sufficient for you, for My strength is made perfect in weakness.' The time was now.

I talked it over with Redemia, who was instantly enthusiastic and eager to go ahead. But one thing was immediately obvious: we couldn't do it with just the two of us. It was impossible for two young girls to run a rehabilitation home for ex-prisoners; there would have to be a man to oversee the work.

Straight away I thought of Dondie, who often helped James at church, taking Bible studies and leading adult Sunday school. He'd been with us on prison visits a number of times and was always keen to help with any kind of evangelism and outreach. Dondie was working very successfully as a freelance land agent, earning commission on the plots of building land he sold, and was clearly very intelligent and capable. His spiritual maturity was plain to see in the way he taught the Scriptures. He seemed suitable in every way and I was sure he was the right man for the job.

I had learned caution, however, and I admitted to myself that in the few months I'd known him I had come to like and admire Dondie a great deal. He was one of those people whose personalities make them the centre of any group of which they're a part, but his popularity hadn't made him conceited. At thirty-one, he was slightly older than most of the young people at church and was often on the receiving end of jokes about his age and the fact that he was still single. He took this with perfect good humour, as he did when they teased him about his deep voice and his height (he was quite short). If Dondie were to join us in the work, it had to be in response to a call from God, not because I wanted it, so when I approached him I would have to exclude the least hint of persuasion on my part. When, therefore, I asked Dondie to pray as to whether it were God's will for him to work in the Philippine Outreach Centre rehabilitation home, I was careful to spell out the level of commitment that would be involved. It would be his job to live in the home with the ex-prisoners and conduct daily Bible studies with them. 'There'll be no salary,' I explained, 'but we'll give you what we can, according to what God provides.'

Good jobs were not so plentiful that a Filipino would lightly give up his career prospects to take on such hard work and responsibility for no salary. I had done my best to ensure that Dondie would accept only if he believed God was calling him. He agreed to pray.

Redemia and I, meanwhile, wasted no time and began to look for suitable premises. We had very little money. I was still receiving my regular support from the congregation at the Upper Room and had been given an extra gift of £1,000 by a friend of my mother, but that had gone towards the purchase of a small car – a twenty-year-old VW Beetle – which we increasingly needed as the work expanded. We decided that Redemia should be the one to search for a property, as Filipinos always ask higher prices from foreigners, imagining them all to be rich. I stayed at home and prayed.

On the first day, Redemia returned wearily after several hours, having had no success. Rents in Subic were very high. So many US servicemen from the naval base were renting houses in the town that property owners were able to demand exorbitant amounts. Redemia asked whether I would consider having the rehabilitation home in Castillejos, a small town just to the north of Subic. It was only a ten-minute jeepney ride away from our bungalow in Pamatawan, which, being on the edge of Subic, was as close to

Castillejos as it was to Subic town centre. It seemed a possible solution, so I agreed.

Next day, Redemia returned home beaming. 'Chrissy, I've seen just the place, a bungalow in Castillejos, and the rent's only 400 pesos a month!'

When I went back with her to look at it, I could see why it was so cheap. It had been empty for quite a while and looked very dilapidated. There was no guttering or drainage, no running water, and the roof needed repairing. But it was only 400 pesos, and I always enjoyed a challenge. Inside, there was a good-sized living and dining room, one large bedroom, three smaller bedrooms, a typically Filipino kitchen with a sink but no running water, and a bathroom with nothing in it except a toilet and a hole in the floor for drainage.

We went home and prayed about it. I had no specific, audible word from the Lord, but as we prayed I felt an inner conviction and peace that he was guiding us to Castillejos. At the same time, I knew that it would be a temporary location; not the accomplishment of my vision but a stepping stone towards it.

When I began negotiating with the owner of the bungalow, he was initially unwilling to do any maintenance work on the property, as the rent was so low, but after some persuasion and the offer of a slight increase in the rent he changed his mind and agreed that responsibility for maintenance would be his. Things were falling into place. When Dondie came and told me he believed he was being directed to accept the job, this seemed further confirmation that we were truly in the will of God.

Now that I had a definite prospect to offer them, I went again in search of Rhey and Ning. They had moved from the derelict house where I'd visited them before and were now living in one small room in someone else's home. Ning was expecting another baby and was several months into her pregnancy, but as there was no free ante-natal care available, she would only know for sure when the baby was due on the day she actually went into labour.

I'd brought some sweets for Nina, the younger of their two girls. Precy, because of her illness, was fed only on condensed milk. As I leaned over to offer some *banana-que* (like toffee apples, but made with bananas) to Nina, Precy suddenly grabbed it and in a few seconds had eaten it all. She was obviously ravenous. Gently, I asked Rhey and Ning how they were managing to feed Precy. They looked at the floor and in a halting voice Rhey told me that they frequently had no money for food, even ordinary food for themselves, and milk was so expensive they could rarely afford it. While there was usually a neighbour willing to give them a bit of rice, getting hold of milk was not so easy. Rhey loved Precy very much. Though she was now about seven, he still referred to her as his baby and I could hardly imagine the pain it must be causing him to see her so hungry.

Glad to be able to bring a little hope into their grim situation, I told them the good news about the rehabilitation home. They were elated at the prospect of security and regular food for the children. When I left, I asked Rhey to walk with me to the town centre, where I could buy him a supply of milk for Precy.

The image of the frail, starving child haunted me, and when, a few days later, Rhey came to see me I knew before he spoke what he was going to say. 'Sister Chrissy, Precy is dead.'

I tried to comfort him, reminding him that his innocent little girl was safe in the Lord's hands and would never suffer again. For Ning, who was not yet a Christian, there could be no such consolation. I wept for them both.

Rhey also faced difficulties in arranging the funeral, for which he had no money. I gave him what I could and agreed to conduct a short service for Precy. We were into the rainy season and on the day of the funeral, the downpour was torrential. Several of Rhey's relatives, whom I'd never met before, came to the service at his sister's house and when it was over we set off on the long walk up the mountainside to the cemetery. Public cemeteries, where the poor can be buried free of charge, are mostly situated a long way from the main roads, as land is cheap there. Ning's pregnancy was too advanced to allow her to make the journey and I walked at Rhey's side, weeping with him for his loss, but also for joy that Precy's suffering was over. The rain mingled with our tears as we climbed.

Meanwhile, the contract for the house at Castillejos had been signed and we began the task of turning the building into a home. The young people at church eagerly volunteered to form a cleaning party and turned up in a laughing crowd, wearing their oldest clothes and with handkerchiefs on their heads, all ready for work. They tackled the scrubbing and sweeping with determination and my heart lifted as I worked alongside them, feeling how good it was to be part of a fellowship where we were friends and not just members of the same church. In a remarkably short time the accumulated dirt and grime were gone and once a coat or two of paint had been put on, the place began to look habitable. Apart from the fact that there was no furniture.

Mom and Pop Houghton had introduced me to a number of Christians on the naval base, and one of these, who ran a Bible study group, invited me along to give my testimony and talk about my work. I told them of our plans for the rehabilitation home, and the generous people on the base donated several pieces of furniture and lots of other household goods. Mom and Pop also put me in touch with a Christian carpenter who had done work for them at the Military Mission, and he made us some bunk beds and a dining table. By September we were ready to go.

We fixed a day to celebrate the completion of the home with a thanksgiving service. I invited Pop Houghton to speak and to dedicate the building to the Lord, and as always he was full of words of encouragement. At the end of the day, we all shared a typically Filipino feast. There was rice (there was always rice!), chicken cooked with black pepper, bay leaves and potatoes, and barbecued fish stuffed with tomatoes and onions. We lingered over the food, enjoying the fellowship and talking over our plans for the future.

Rhey and his family moved in immediately, as did Jason, along with Dondie as overseer. Every day they met for Bible study, at which Dondie and I shared responsibility for the teaching, and for discussion of their spiritual needs. On one occasion, Rhey told us that he was praying that the expected baby would be a son; he'd promised the Lord that he would 'go straight' for the rest of his life if the Lord would grant his request.

One Sunday after church a few weeks later, I went with Dondie and Jason to the rehab (the rehabilitation home had become 'the rehab' to all of us) to find that Ning was just delivering her baby right there in the house. The local midwife was helping her. Rhey came rushing out to us, yelling, 'It's a boy, it's a boy!' before dashing back inside. Meanwhile, the midwife was telling Ning not to stop pushing, as there was another baby to come. Ning had had no idea she was carrying twins. Minutes later Rhey ran out again, 'It's another boy, another boy!' Needless to say, he was euphoric. The Lord had given him not one son, but two!

More than ten years have passed since then, and Rhey has never forgotten the promise he made to the Lord. For him this has meant living with poverty, but he has never considered returning to the drug dealing which once made him a rich man. He is a living testimony to the grace of God.

In order to encourage Rhey and Jason to share their faith, I began to involve them in the prison outreach. I didn't take them to Iba or Camp Maquinaya, as I judged they were not yet ready to visit the jails where they had been inmates themselves. However, I occasionally made trips to the big main prison at Muntinlupa, Manila. During my first ten months in the Philippines, friends in England had put me in touch with a remarkable American woman who had been working with the inmates at Muntinlupa for thirty years. Her name was Olga Robertson, but she was known to everyone as 'Mammie Olga'. An account of her experiences would fill volumes.

Muntinlupa is actually a district in Manila, but the name has become synonymous with the prison located there. It is the most notorious prison in the Philippines and consists of a vast campus on which are sited three separate prison buildings housing up to 12,000 inmates. The maximum security prison is called New Bilibid and the medium security, Sampaguita, and it was in these two that Mammie Olga worked; there is also a minimum security facility. The campus is almost a self-contained community, comprising, along with the prison buildings, houses for those who work in the prisons (Mammie Olga had one of these), schools, and churches established by both Roman Catholics and the various Protestant denominations. There are also churches actually within the prisons themselves. Mammie Olga had founded churches for the inmates in both New Bilibid and Sampaguita and over the years had seen many of them become Christians. She would train the converts to take responsibility for the preaching and pastoral oversight of the congregations, and after finishing their sentences several of them stayed on to help her with the work.

Mammie was greatly loved by the inmates and her long and faithful service had earned her the respect of all the prison officers. Though security at Muntinlupa was much stricter than at Camp Maquinaya, the mere mention of her name was enough to secure admittance. Mammie was (and still is) a source of inspiration to me, and I loved the opportunity to share in her ministry when I visited.

The first time I took Rhey and Jason with me, even Rhey confessed he was scared. Muntinlupa is exclusively for convicted prisoners and contains some of the worst criminals in the Philippines. But after meeting the Christian inmates and seeing some of these very men now making an uncompromising stand for Christ and even learning to be pastors and teachers, both Rhey and Jason came away with an increased faith that they too could put the past behind them and live for Christ. Ministry among ex-prisoners isn't all about happy endings, however. Our requirement for admission to the rehab was not conversion to Christ, simply a desire to forsake crime, but we found that those who had no interest in the things of God usually left of their own accord before long, unable to resist the lure of their former lives. One such was Danilo Cruz.

Danilo came to us in November, a few months after the rehab opened, just as I was due to leave for a three-month furlough in England. My next news of him came in the shape of a letter from Dondie some six weeks later. It seemed that Danilo, though he had professed interest in the gospel, had found the pull of the world stronger than his desire to be reconciled to God, and had left the rehab after a couple of weeks. Three weeks after that, his head was found in a box on a bus, with a stick of marijuana stuffed into his mouth. We never found out who did it, or why.

If only men would realise how transient are the pleasures of the world, while the consequences of rejecting Christ are for ever. And what an urgent task we have as Christians to warn them. Serving the Lord can involve suffering, but with eternal issues at stake can we allow it to deter us?

11

Confusion

By the time I returned to England in November 1985, Dondie had become quite special to me. We spent a great deal of time in each other's company, both at the rehab, where we shared the Bible teaching, and in the jails, where Dondie now did much of the interpreting for me. Since, however, I had no reason to think he returned my feelings, I'd kept my own well hidden. I wrote to him a few times while I was away, but apart from his letter telling me about Danilo, which was quite impersonal and businesslike, I didn't hear from him at all. I decided I would have to accept the fact that Dondie had no interest in me except as a colleague.

At the same time, I'd been seeing rather a lot of Stuart. Despite our broken engagement four years earlier we had remained friends and he had been very supportive of my work. He was much more stable spiritually than in our teenage years and was now an elder and assistant treasurer at the Upper Room.

As on my previous furlough, I had received many invitations to speak about my work, and Stuart often volunteered to drive me to these engagements, which took me all over the country. He was kind to me in other ways, taking me out for meals or to the theatre, wanting me to enjoy for a

short time some of the things I'd given up by going to the
Philippines. It was impossible not to enjoy being treated
with such consideration, but my pleasure in Stuart's company was disturbed by the uneasy awareness that spending
so much time with him was beginning to reawaken the
feelings I'd had for him before, especially when, as we
inevitably did, we talked about the time when we had
been engaged. I was troubled by the unexpected turn my
emotions were taking and wondered what was going on in
Stuart's mind, though, overtly at least, the understanding
was that we were just friends. Until the week before I was
due to go back.

We were reminiscing about the past, swapping memories
of our courtship, when Stuart said tentatively, 'We could
still get married if you wanted to.'

Hopes I'd thought were long dead rose up again to
dazzle me. Everything I had wanted, everything I had
wept for when our engagement ended, was being offered
me; all the broken dreams which had driven me to dieting
and anorexia could be made whole again. How desperately
I longed to snatch at this chance of happiness. But even
while part of me reached out with delight towards the
future which my imagination was already busily painting
– flowers, romantic walks in the park, returning from an
exotic honeymoon to a beautiful home of our own – I felt
again the sharp tug of unease. What about my vision for the
Philippine Outreach Centre? How could I marry Stuart
without renouncing the work to which I knew God had
called me?

Tearfully I told Stuart it was impossible. Our lives were
moving in different directions; mine to the Philippines, his
towards the managing of his own very successful engineering company. Of course, Stuart could see perfectly
well that I was refusing him because I felt I ought to, not
because I didn't want him, and he himself saw no difficulty in reconciling our marriage with my call to the
mission field: I would spend three months every year in

the Philippines and his business would pay for my trips and finance the ministry. He was so sure it would work, and I wanted to think so too. But was it what God wanted for us? Satan had tried so many times to deflect me from obeying God, and I had no assurance that this was his will for me. I told Stuart I couldn't make any commitment to him until the Lord confirmed that it was right.

I tried hard in the days that followed to convince myself that it was, but all my efforts failed to stifle a deep-seated sense of misgiving. Our time together was almost over. Even before I left, Stuart was flying to Switzerland for a skiing holiday. He remained full of his plan, confident that God would confirm it, and as we talked it seemed to grow more plausible. But I still had no assurance from the Lord.

On one of our last days together, Stuart suddenly said, 'Why don't we go and look at rings?'

I knew I shouldn't allow myself to be drawn so far towards a commitment to him when I was so confused, but he persuaded me that if he bought me a ring, I needn't wear it until I was certain our relationship was right. He would be willing to wait and we could postpone any announcement of our engagement until I was sure. I found myself standing beside him in the jeweller's shop, trying on a beautiful diamond ring. As I looked at my finger where the stone flashed and sparkled, I felt like the star of a Hollywood film. That was the trouble. I had the sense of being caught up in all the romance and all the unreality of that celluloid world.

When Stuart left for Switzerland I went with him to the airport and cried uncontrollably all the way. I couldn't tell him of my fears that my dreams would come to nothing.

Days later I returned to a different world. Which was to be the real world for me? That of expensive clothes, dinner dates, carpeted churches and Sunday roasts? Or was it to be heat rash, perspiration, hard wooden benches and fish with rice? Could Stuart be right – was it really possible to achieve a compromise, to keep a foot in both worlds?

By the time I'd been back a few weeks, Stuart's plan had lost much of its plausibility. I began to fear that my ability to accept the conditions in the Philippines depended on regarding them as the norm. If I spent nine months of every year in England, my time in the Philippines would become an unnatural and unwelcome interruption of my accustomed way of life and I could end up resenting both the people and the place. My work would be impossible under those circumstances. How could I reach people for Christ if I couldn't enter fully into their culture and identify with them? Yet marriage to Stuart represented everything the woman in me had ever hoped for.

Even though I was incapable of reaching a firm decision, I felt I had to tell Dondie about the possibility of my engagement, because it would affect the future running of the Philippine Outreach Centre if it ever became reality. He took the news quietly, though I had the distinct impression that he disapproved, which naturally did nothing to ease my turmoil. My indecision was compounded when the reason for his disapproval emerged a few days later, as we were on our way to one of the jails in the old Beetle. The car broke down and as we waited for the mechanic, the topic of my engagement came up again. Dondie stunned me by saying, 'Well, I have feelings for you too.'

Here was something else to add to my confusion! Why hadn't he spoken earlier? (It was a long time before I had the answer to that one.) And what did 'feelings' actually mean? I didn't feel up to tackling these large questions and instead seized on something more immediate and concrete. 'Then why didn't you answer my letters?' I asked.

It turned out that he'd never received them and the letters he'd written to me must also have gone astray. What a muddle it all was.

Dondie and I said no more on that occasion, but I

brooded endlessly on the possible significance of his revelation. Could it be that the Lord was telling me that Dondie had been brought into my life to be more than just a co-worker? Was this why I had no assurance about Stuart? I began to feel I had been unfair to Stuart in allowing him to commit himself to waiting for me. Yet the alternative was to give him up completely. . . . My thoughts ground on like a remorseless treadmill, going round and round but getting nowhere.

Competing for my attention with the seemingly intractable problem of my own future was my anxiety about Redemia's. Several months previously Redemia had met Sammy, a young American serviceman, and they were instantly attracted. By the time Sammy had to return to America two weeks later, Redemia was head over heels in love. They wrote to each other every day and soon Redemia was talking about marriage. But Sammy wasn't a Christian. She'd met him when he was visiting the home of our landlord, who lived in the house next to ours and was himself, though a Filipino by birth, a retired US serviceman.

For the first time, Redemia and I had a serious disagreement as I tried to convince her that it would be wrong to marry a man who was a non-believer. From my own bitter experience with Simon, I knew what it was to be swept along by emotion into a wrong relationship, and I didn't want Redemia to make the same mistake. But she was adamant, and by the time I returned from England in February plans for her wedding in America were well advanced. Now I had to come to terms with the fact that I was soon to lose Redemia, my closest friend on whom I'd depended for so much.

Meanwhile, work had to go on. We were visiting Camp Maquinaya twice a week now and Iba once, on top of running the rehab where adult residents now numbered five, including Rhey, Ning and Jason as well as Rhey's three children. Every morning after an early breakfast, while Ning cleaned the house and cared for the children, the boys would go off to spend the day working on the plot of land we had leased nearby. They were growing various kinds of fruit and vegetables, which was both a healthy occupation for them and a useful contribution to the domestic economy of the rehab. In the evenings I usually joined them for prayer and Bible study, and of course we all went together to the Born-Again Christians' Den on Sundays.

Shortly after my return, we added pig-keeping to our activities – an enterprise made possible because the owner of our vegetable plot offered us the use of his pigsties. We started off with just a few pigs, two of which represented a very special gift I'd received while in England. A number of the churches and fellowships to whom I'd spoken about my work had begun to support me financially, and among these was a small group of elderly women in Sale, near my home town of Altrincham. One of them, Amy, had taught herself to knit and made dishcloths which she sold to raise funds for us. 'I know this can't do much,' she said, as she handed me the money she had raised, 'but I hope it will help.'

'You mustn't think that. With this amount we can buy a pig,' I replied. The idea of buying us a pig appealed to her enormously and prompted her friend Alice to ask me to use her money to buy a pig too.

I named two of our first pigs Alice and Amy and we kept them as breeders, raising others to provide meat for the rehab kitchen. In succeeding years, Alice and Amy's off-spring continued to supply us both with food and with piglets to sell when money was tight.

I received another invitation to Bohol, to speak at the annual convention at Pastor Thomas' Bible school in Tag-bilaran. As I'd done on my first trip to Bohol, I planned the journey so as to include a short visit to the children's mission at Sunshine Corner on the island of Cebu. I'd promised Jason that he could come with me on my next trip and since it would offend Filipino notions of propriety for a single woman to travel alone with a single man of similar age, Dondie came with us too. I was apprehensive about spending so much time with him (we'd be away for two weeks), but unless I were to disappoint Jason, who was very keen to come, there was no other way. Besides, though I was reasonably proficient in Tagalog by now, I still needed an interpreter for preaching, and Dondie's presence meant we would be able to take any opportunities that offered of visiting the jails.

As flights for three of us would be too expensive, we had to travel by boat, so on the day of our departure we set off for Manila Bay, leaving Rhey to oversee the day-to-day running of the rehab and Redemia to supervise the Bible studies. Seen from the land, the boat on which we were to make the twenty-four-hour journey to Cebu looked like a typical, if ancient, cross-channel ferry, but once on board the resemblance ended abruptly.

'Dondie,' I asked, 'what are we supposed to sit on?'

'Oh, there are no seats, just cots.'

Cots? Cots were for babies, I thought. When we went down to the dormitories I had my second taste of culture shock in the Philippines: the 'cots' were actually double bunk beds. Travelling alone, I might have ended up sleeping next to anyone. 'Imagine writing home,' I thought, 'and telling them I'd slept with all these people. What would Mum think if I told her I'd slept with Dondie and Jason? Anyway, I don't care! I'd rather sleep with someone I know next to me than a perfect stranger.'

Being the only white person in the dormitory, however, made me very conspicuous and earned me an embarrassing amount of attention from the other passengers. How could I lie down and sleep with everyone watching me? I hung on to my dignity for as long as possible, but tiredness won in the end and I stretched out on my bunk to get what rest I could. At least we were travelling second class; the third-class passengers ate and slept in the aisles, so there were bodies everywhere.

My discomfort increased as the journey went on. The food available on the boat was both expensive and badly prepared, so most people had brought pots of rice, fish and vegetables, whose mingled smells hung heavily in the air, becoming more and more unpleasant as the food began to go off. I was glad I had decided to stick to sandwiches. Towards the end, we were almost suffocated by the stench of sweating bodies, dirty bathrooms, babies' nappies and rotting food.

But the few days we spent at Sunshine Corner more than repaid the effort of getting there. Sunshine Corner was in the city of Cebu (the island and its main city share the same name) and was a mission for street kids. When it opened its doors at 5 o'clock each evening, anything between twenty and forty dirty, tired, hungry children would come streaming through. Well acquainted with the routine, they headed straight for the bathroom, where one of the workers would check that they were scrubbed clean, delousing them where necessary, while another collected all the dirty clothes, which went immediately into the washing machine.

Then, dressed in fresh Sunshine Corner clothes, the children waited for the call to dinner. I've never seen kids run as fast as they did when the summons came. Huge piles of rice, corn grits, fish and fresh fruit were demolished in short order and every plate scraped clean. Bible hour followed, then prayers, by which point the younger ones had already drifted off to sleep and by 8 o'clock the mats were brought out and all the children settled down for the night.

Early next day, after morning prayers and a huge breakfast, their own clothes were returned to them clean and dry, and they were ready for another day on the streets. To my mind, the great virtue of this mission lay in its willingness to respond to the kids' needs: the streets were their life and they would never have submitted to the discipline of a conventional children's home. Sunshine Corner took the gospel to children who could be reached no other way.

Our visit to the larger of Cebu's two jails turned out to be a memorable occasion. When we went to request permission to conduct a service, we took with us one of the Sunshine Corner workers, Luke, who had once been detained there himself. We had no trouble obtaining the warden's consent, but we were made to wait for a long time before being admitted; the inmates were preparing for us, the guards explained. When at last we were allowed in we were greeted by the sight of 700 men jammed shoulder to shoulder on the jail's basketball court: every single inmate had wanted to be present. This was, and still is, a very rare occurrence.

Luke spoke first, weeping as he told how, in that very jail, he had heard of the love of Christ and accepted him as his Saviour. A stillness that was almost palpable came over the men as they listened, and when I stood up to preach from the Scriptures the quality of their attention was such that I felt I was speaking directly to each member of that tightly packed crowd. Dondie closed the service by asking any who wished to accept Christ to raise their hands. Literally hundreds responded. I just stood and wept, my mind going back to the FGBMFI convention in Glasgow many years ago when the Lord told me I would one day be used to minister to many people. I won't know until I meet him how many of those men stood firm for Christ, but it was a joy to bring them God's word that day. And a good note on which to end our time in Cebu.

Another boat – but only eight hours this time. However, as the journey to Bohol was shorter, both the boat and the cots were correspondingly smaller. Eight hours can seem a long time.

On arriving at Tagbilaran, we were introduced to 'Mammie Ruth', a lady in her fifties whom everyone seemed to know. I gathered that she was the Mammie Olga of the southern Philippines. Mammie Ruth was also a guest speaker at Thomas' convention and I was to share a room with her.

Introductions over, we were set to work at once in true Filipino fashion. As we battled through a hectic programme of church services, prison visits and meetings at the Bible school, the load was lightened for me by the ease with which Dondie and I worked together. We made a good team. We often sang together before I preached and he interpreted. Sometimes, to give me a break, he would take on the preaching himself. But what I lacked was someone to share my emotional burden.

While we had been away from the rehab, Dondie had opened up a little more about his 'feelings' for me, and in spite of his natural reserve I could no longer doubt that what he felt was genuine love. For my part, I was coming to enjoy being with him more and more, not just because of the work we shared but for himself.

These sensations troubled me deeply and I suffered terrible pangs of guilt whenever I thought of Stuart. I was a mystery to myself. I no longer knew what I wanted, nor, more importantly, what the Lord wanted for me. In desperation I confided in Mammie Ruth who, though she couldn't solve my dilemma, none the less greatly comforted me by her assurance that if I waited patiently, God would show me his will.

I was distracted from brooding on the tangled web of my own emotions by Jason's problems. One night, after giving his testimony at a prison service, he had broken down and confessed he was finding it hard to resist the temptation to go back to taking drugs. As we returned to Subic, I reflected that it might be easier to sort out my future if I had more time for myself.

But if I was hoping that the pace would slacken, I was to be disappointed.

12

A City on a Hill

Just when it seemed I most needed the comfort of familiarity, the pattern of my life began to shift. Redemia left for America to be married, and I hadn't even the consolation of feeling confident that all would be well with her. I should have known that the unwelcome change was part of the larger pattern God was weaving, but at the time I simply felt bereft of an intimate friend and valued co-worker.

Dondie now took over entirely the job of interpreting for me in the jails and the gap which was left in our children's work by Redemia's departure was filled by Freda, a middle-aged lady from Peterhead in Scotland, whom Mum had met through her IGO and Hollybush contacts. Freda phoned Mum one day and, right out of the blue, announced that the Lord had told her to go to the Philippines to help me. Having had a troubled childhood herself, spending most of her teenage years in care, Freda had developed a desire to help other needy children; and the timing of her arrival, just before Redemia left, was perfect. Language would be no problem, as she would have as her assistant a local girl from Pamatawan, a neighbour of mine and Redemia's called Joy who, after helping with the children's outreaches for several months, had recently asked to join us.

The last few months had also seen our ministry to young people extend into local schools, such as San Agustin School in Castillejos, where a number of the children in the neighbourhood of the rehab were enrolled. It was a public (government-run) school and catered for both elementary and high school pupils. (Elementary level is the equivalent of English infant and junior school, and high school of English secondary school.) Public schools in the Philippines don't have daily corporate worship, so we ran a Bible hour for elementary pupils after the official end of the school day, while for the high school students we were allowed to do Bible teaching within the school timetable. Of the youngsters who accepted Christ as a result of our outreach there, several are now being used in the Lord's work in pastoral ministry and leading worship in various churches.

Freda worked with us for several months and she and I became good friends during the time we lived together, the gap in our ages being easily spanned by her warmth and sense of humour. She was great fun to be with, and a great asset in the children's outreaches. As time went on, her vision for children's work grew and she conceived the idea of opening a children's home for the street kids of Olongapo, an idea she was able to realise later that year while I was on furlough in England. The home she established is still flourishing and has given a bright new future to many children.

On my journey back to the Philippines, I was intrigued to notice a young woman on the opposite side of the plane reading *Arise and Reap*, a book which I recognised as being by a Christian woman who went to the Philippines as a missionary. When we stopped over in Dubai, we boarded the bus for the terminal together.

'I couldn't help noticing the book you were reading,' I said. 'Are you on your way to the Philippines?'

'Yes, that's right.'

'Me too. What will you be doing there?'

'I'm going to be a missionary.'

'I'm a missionary too! Where will you be working?'

'Subic.'

Her name was Julie and she'd just graduated from Bible school in Peterhead, Freda's home town. She felt God was calling her to the Philippines, but since she wasn't sure in what capacity she should work, or where, the principals of the school had arranged for her to spend some time with Freda, familiarising herself with the country while she prayed and sought the Lord's guidance.

By some mischance, Freda wasn't there to meet her when we landed in Manila, but the Lord had seen to it that I was and we travelled to Subic together. As it was very late when we arrived, I invited her to spend the night in my bungalow. In fact, Julie continued to stay with me for the rest of her visit since the house Freda had taken wasn't really big enough to accommodate another person.

Meanwhile, the bungalow at Castillejos which housed the rehab was strained to bursting point. Ning's sister had joined us and numbers swelled considerably with the advent of Freddie and Peter, ex-prisoners from Camp Maquinaya; Peter also brought his wife and four children and their fifth child was born in the rehab. I had known from the start that this building was a temporary stepping stone and it began to look as if the Lord would soon be moving us on.

Another consequence of growing numbers was the difficulty of transporting all the rehab residents to the Born-Again Christians' Den every Sunday. My old Beetle was beginning to feel her age and objected to the constant overloading during the forty-minute journey – which would take an hour by public transport and might be lengthened by a further hour of waiting on the return trip, as the bus wouldn't leave Olongapo until it was full.

Could it be that the second phase of my vision was about

to unfold? Was it now God's time to establish a worshipping community for the rehab members? Dondie and I began to pray and seek the Lord, and he gave both of us the confirmation that we should go ahead with the Philippine Outreach Christian Fellowship.

We planned to meet in my home in Pamatawan. In retrospect, it seems odd that I never once considered using the rehab house in Castillejos, which on the surface was a more suitable venue in terms of size, but the decision was undoubtedly prompted by the Lord, who had given me my original vision in and for Subic. Being on the northern edge of Subic, and equidistant from the centre of Subic and Castillejos, my home provided a meeting place both consistent with the vision and conveniently close to the rehab. Its smallness wasn't an insuperable problem: by moving out all the furniture each Sunday and replacing it with bench seating, we reckoned we could manage. A local man in Pamatawan made the benches for us, and we were ready to go.

On the morning of 2nd November 1986, when we held our first service, the house was filled with people. All the rehab residents were there and Joy, who of course came from Pamatawan, had invited several members of her family. A number of local people, whom we didn't know, also joined us. As I welcomed them, my excitement was tinged with nervousness. When the Lord gave me the vision of founding a church, I hadn't expected that I would be its pastor, yet in a short while I would be standing up before these people to preach God's word. I knew he had given me the ability to preach and I was willing to use the gift in obedience to him, but as a woman it felt strange to be doing so in this situation. Dondie had little experience of preaching, but his ability as a Bible teacher would be indispensable in the adult Sunday school which would normally precede the service. Between us we had the necessary gifts to meet the congregation's needs.

After the opening praise and worship and Scripture

reading, I got up and, with Dondie interpreting, began to preach the good news of salvation through Christ. The Holy Spirit was with us that morning and several of the non-Christians responded by surrendering their lives to the Lord. I have a vivid memory of one local woman weeping in repentance while trying to comfort her three-year-old son who was crying in bewilderment at his mother's tears. The new converts were eager to learn and soon we were having church Bible studies and prayer meetings midweek, each as well attended as the Sunday services.

Another of our earliest converts was Joseph, whom I invited to church when he was released on bail from Camp Maquinaya, where he was being detained on charges of possession of drugs and drug pushing. Though he was initially reluctant to come, and despite the unpromising character of his first visit – it was at a prayer meeting, and he arrived thoroughly drunk – there was no mistaking the genuineness of the profession of repentance and faith which he made on his second visit. The evidence was the transformation of his life and his determination to give up drugs for good.

We accepted him into the rehab and I went, as I often did on behalf of prisoners, to see the judge responsible for his case and ask when the hearing was likely to be. I took the opportunity to tell the judge of the change that had taken place in him and that he had voluntarily entered the rehab. When the case came up, Joseph realised that he faced the possibility of ten years in jail, or even longer, and it was therefore with profound thankfulness for the grace of God that he heard his sentence pronounced: he was put on probation for six years and ordered to report regularly to his probation officer. I knew then that God had heard David Chaudhary's prayer that I would 'find favour with the authorities'.

Though we were delighted to welcome Joseph into the rehab, the problem of overcrowding in our 'stepping stone' was becoming ever more pressing. If the work were to expand, we would have to move.

One day towards the end of November, Julie went out walking with Joy, exploring parts of Subic she'd never seen before, and returned scarcely able to contain her excitement. 'Chrissy! We've just seen a building in Calapandayan that could be just what you need – an old empty hospital, really big. Will you come and have a look?'

I had lived in Subic for three years and had never even heard of the existence of such a building in the *barangay* of Calapandayan. I had no idea what to expect, but I was willing to explore every avenue, so I got the car out and drove back with Julie. The hospital was situated right on top of a steep hill so we parked the car at the bottom and started to climb.

As soon as the building came into view, I said, 'This is it. This is the vision the Lord gave me.' When I looked down into the valley below, I could see Subic's 'red-light' district where, in my first months in the Philippines, I'd been shocked to see half-dressed girls running along the street calling to American GIs and trying to drag them into one of the row of dingy bars. A verse of Scripture came into my mind: 'You are the light of the world. A city that is set on a hill cannot be hidden' (Mt 5:14). I prayed that our light would shine in that needy place.

On closer inspection the hospital proved to be truly enormous – bigger even than the General Hospital in Olongapo. It had three storeys and we estimated that there must be close to a hundred rooms. Just opposite was a single-storey building in the shape of a squat 'L', which had been a training school for nurses. It is amazing how different things can seem when viewed through the eyes of faith. To me these buildings were beautiful, though in reality they had lain empty and untended for years and bore the marks of many strong typhoons. They needed literally millions of pesos' worth of renovation.

As we were leaving we met a man who lived nearby and I

asked him if he knew who owned the building. He'd heard that it had been repossessed by a local bank, so I went straight there to make enquiries, only to find that my information was wrong. It hadn't been repossessed and no one at the bank knew the owner. They did know, however, that he had a mortgage and made monthly repayments to the SSS (the Social Security System which, in addition to dealing with such things as pensions, also makes loans to its members). So it was on to the SSS in Manila.

Since Dondie knew Manila better than I, he came with me and successfully located the SSS building where the staff, having consulted their records, gave us the name of the estate agent who dealt with the property. When we reached the agency we discovered that its owner, Mr Cruz, was also the owner of the hospital. What a relief. On asking to speak to him, we were told we would have to wait, and the interval certainly provided food for thought. Every so often, an employee would enter Mr Cruz's office, to emerge minutes later with a shattered expression and sweat pouring down his face.

Satan started to whisper: 'Chrissy, this is one hard businessman and you're making a big mistake.' Another man left the office looking pulverised. 'You're going to talk to him about buying his building when you've no money? You're a fool.'

'Don't you ever give up?' I retorted. 'The Lord can supply all my need.'

Even Dondie was nervous. 'What if he has us thrown out?'

'So what? What do we have to lose? We won't exactly be losing our best friend. Anyway, if God is for us, who can be against us?'

Eventually we were led into the office and introduced ourselves to the formidable Mr Cruz. After a few minutes of preliminary chitchat about England, which Mr Cruz, who seemed to have business interests all over Europe, had visited many times, he invited us to explain the purpose of our visit. Since this concerned my vision, Dondie left the talking to me and I began to tell Mr Cruz about the work of the Philippine Outreach Centre.

'Yes, yes,' he interrupted, 'this is all very nice, but what has it to do with me?'

'We've been looking for bigger premises,' I explained, 'and came across your hospital in Calapandayan. I'm here, sir, to ask how much you're selling it for.'

'How much are you offering?'

'Well, actually, I haven't any money at the moment. I'm . . . .'

My voice was drowned by Mr Cruz's roar of laughter. 'You mean to tell me you've come to buy my building without any money? Who do you think is going to pay for it? The Queen of England?'

'No, sir, the King of kings.'

'You must really be somebody,' he said, puzzled and intrigued rather than sarcastic, 'to come here and ask to buy a building with no money. You must really be somebody.'

I whispered a word of praise to the Lord. There I was, before a millionaire, and he was saying I was somebody. Well, of course, I was nothing in myself, but as I'd learned long ago, our God is a God who does everything with our nothing, takes it and fills it with himself so that the powerful of this world can see that, in him, we are 'somebody'.

'I'll tell you what,' he went on, 'seeing that you have no money, let's not talk about the hospital. There's the nurses' training school. I'll let you have the use of that first. There are thirty-three hectares of land around those buildings that you can use for your pigs and agriculture and any other livelihood projects. If you want to renovate the school, it's up to you; we can talk about the hospital later.'

There had been no mention so far of any rent or leasing arrangement, without which we would not have the security of a contract. Trusting the Lord doesn't excuse us from using the common sense he has given us, so I asked how much the rent would be.

'Whatever you're paying now for your own home and your current rehabilitation home. If you all move into the school you'll have no extra expenses. Come back in a few days to pay the deposit and sign the contract.'

'But I can't live in the rehabilitation home myself,' I objected.

'Well,' he said, easily, 'you can have one of my properties at La Sirena beach. Go and have a look, pick whichever you like. I own the whole beach resort there. Tell my secretary at La Sirena when you've decided; she'll deal with it.'

Could this be the same man who reduced his staff to jelly? The Lord was surely with us that day. Just before we left, however, we caught a glimpse of the hard business-man whose ruthlessness had been in abeyance during the interview so far. 'I must warn you,' he said, 'that I can be your best friend or your worst enemy.' I could well believe it, but my trust was in the Lord.

I left the office completely awed. My intention had been simply to find out how much money to pray for. Instead, I came away with everything fixed for us to move into the nurses' school.

The beach resort at La Sirena consisted of a hotel, a restaurant, sports facilities, and a number of very pretty beach cottages, much like my own bungalow. But it was not really near enough to the hospital. When I mentioned this to Mr Cruz's secretary, she pointed out that he also owned houses at the bottom of the hill, below the hospital; why didn't I ask for one of these?

I returned to Mr Cruz's office a few days later to sign the contract. Emboldened by the success of our previous inter-view, I explained to him that though I had enough for the deposit, we needed all our available funds to renovate the building. Without demur, he agreed to waive the deposit. The secretary dealing with the paperwork was so taken aback that she asked him to confirm that everything was in order. 'He's never done this before,' she told me. 'Our policy is to insist on a minimum of two months' rent in advance.'

Before I left, Mr Cruz, affability well to the fore, asked me, 'Is there anything else you want?'

'Well, there's just one thing,' I replied, feeling a bit like Oliver Twist. 'The houses at La Sirena are lovely, but it's too far from the hospital. I really need something nearer.'

Before I could go on, he broke in: 'At the bottom of the hill there, you will see several houses, all my property. Pick any you want.'

I left the office walking on air.

Preparations for moving began at once as Mr Cruz had insisted on us taking over the properties almost immediately. Julie missed the excitement of the move as she'd gone to Manila to meet David Nellist and spend some time working with him before returning to the UK. As I thought about Julie, I reviewed the events which had led us to the new rehab: Redemia leaving, to be replaced by Freda, because of whom Julie had come to Subic and found the hospital. All strands in God's larger plan.

It would be a wrench to leave my neat little bungalow in Pamatawan, with its bright garden full of flowers which Redemia had planted and carefully tended. My new home, which I would share with Joy, was in a sad state of disrepair, with no glass in the windows, no electricity and no water supply. I had to remind myself of the apostle Paul's instruction: 'Set your mind on things above, not on things on the earth' (Col 3:2). This kind of discipline is particularly necessary in the age we live in, where the pleasures of the world have never presented a stronger temptation to Christians. Without constant vigilance we can be so easily lured away from our calling to live for God and sink into self-indulgence. Of course, material prosperity, if regarded as held in trust from God, to be used in his service, can be a great blessing, but it's up to us to see that we don't turn God's blessing into a curse.

So, setting my mind on the vision the Lord had given me, I was able to turn my back on the comfort and security of my bungalow. Indeed, my loss dwindled into insignificance when seen in the context of all that had to be done at the new rehab. Mr Cruz's insistence on immediate occupation posed enormous problems, as the nurses' school was totally uninhabitable, except by the large ugly lizards, mosquitoes and cockroaches which had colonised it while it lay empty. The interior would have to be entirely rebuilt because every inch of wood had been eaten away by termites. The cement floor was buried under a thick layer of silt washed in from the mountainside every rainy season; spread over an area of almost 500 square yards, that was going to be an awful lot of dirt to clear away. There was no glass in the windows and until all the wiring was renewed, there would be no electricity. More important, it would take a great deal of work to lay on a water supply because the building was so far away from the town's water mains.

My new home, by contrast, though badly in need of repair, could quickly be made habitable at a pinch. Furthermore, there was a natural well nearby, where it would be possible to drill for water, which could be drawn up by a hand pump. Until there was a water supply at the rehab, therefore, though it was a far from ideal arrangement, most of the rehab members would have to be squeezed into the house with Joy and me, apart from a couple of the lads who camped out in the rehab itself.

It took a week of drilling to reach the water level and install the hand pump. We connected a hosepipe to the pump and draped the other end of the pipe through the bathroom window into a large bucket, and after ten minutes of pumping it was possible to have a 'bath'. The water wasn't very clean, though, and was full of long, thin worms, which made bathing an itchy business.

Primitive it may have been, but it was an inexpressible relief after a week in which I had to walk across a field to a nearby well every time I wanted a bath. It wasn't the sort of picturesque well from which Jack and Jill might have fetched a pail of water, either. It was just a point where water sprang up from the ground, in full view of several neighbouring houses. The villagers could hardly be expected not to relish the novel spectacle of a white woman bathing fully clothed by the well – it needed the skill of a contortionist – and the whole thing was an embarrassing ordeal. I much preferred the worms. The water at the house was no good for drinking, of course, but kind neighbours who had a clean supply allowed us to draw water from their well.

While we were wondering what to do about the electricity, it so happened that Rex, one of the inmates at Iba, was released on bail. Rex was an electrician and willingly agreed to do the rewiring. In a remarkably short time my house had the luxury of electric light, and Rex began work on the rehab. Ronnie Castillo was another answer to prayer when he too was released from Iba. Ronnie was acquitted of a murder charge after being involved with several others in a fight in which one man was killed. He'd never shown much interest in the gospel, but he was anxious to find work and as a carpenter he was just what we were looking for. All the wood in the rehab would have to be replaced as and when we could afford it, but Ronnie began by salvaging some usable plywood from the ceilings with which to begin constructing a few temporary bedrooms. He moved into one of these himself, with his wife and three children, having asked to join the rehab a week or so after starting work.

Between the work at the rehab and visits to Iba and Camp Maquinaya, life had never been busier, yet we always made room for our Bible studies and prayer meetings with the rehab members. Though most of them had made a profession of faith in Christ, their knowledge of God's word was at best fragmentary and their eagerness to learn was heartwarming. But my satisfaction with their spiritual progress was marred by the fact that, unlike several other church members, none of the ex-prisoners had received the baptism in the Holy Spirit and seemed not to understand their need of it. Remembering my own inability to live the Christian life prior to baptism in the Spirit, I was only too aware of the struggles they might face in the battle against sin. It never occurred to me that one particularly disastrous failure would shortly pose a threat to me personally.

However, there was no doubt that their faith was increased by the lavish way in which God answered our prayers at this time. The cost of renovation and building materials sometimes stretched our faith to the limits, but the Lord never failed to provide. My network of supporters back home was expanding steadily, so much so that Dad had recently decided to form a charitable trust to administer their contributions. By means of their generous and timely gifts God supplied every single item we prayed for and there was enough to pay a reasonable wage to all those who worked for us.

Looking back over the whole period of renovation, though, perhaps the most remarkable gift came through Mum's efforts. My businessman father was more than a little startled when she took a market stall in Salford and began selling second-hand clothes to raise funds for us. Indefatigable as ever, she single-handedly loaded and unloaded the heavy rails of clothes, and the profit she made was ultimately enough to buy a jeepney, which was invaluable in transporting building materials up the hill to the rehab and which served us for many years afterwards.

Back in the present, meanwhile, there was no lack of employment for everyone. Freddie, Peter and Joseph were all fully occupied and Rhey toiled uncomplainingly up and down the hill carrying water for the reconstruction work until we were able to buy an electric pump for the rehab. The building of a retaining wall to protect against flooding in the rainy season; the construction of new pigsties; the making and installation of a water tank big enough to hold at least a day's supply; the erection of a temporary outside bathroom to serve until we could afford something better: these were just some of the jobs we had to do to make the building viable.

But while all this was still going on, the Philippine Outreach Christian Fellowship had to move into the rehab.

13

'My Times Are in Your Hand'

Because quite a few of the congregation actually lived in Pamatawan, the church had continued to meet there when we moved to the new rehab, first in the home of one of the members and then, because that was too small, in the open air. But soon after we founded the fellowship, another church opened in the same neighbourhood. Its doctrine and practice were fully biblical, yet its existence nevertheless created a problem for us. Many local people drew the conclusion that two separate churches so close together must represent two rival systems. This confusion could only hinder the preaching of the gospel and the obvious solution was for one of us to move elsewhere, but having been in Pamatawan first my natural inclination was to resist being the one to leave. However, as we prayed about it, it became clear that the Lord was directing us to move.

We set about preparing a room in the rehab and I explained the decision to our members in Pamatawan, telling them that they should feel free to join the other church, which would be more convenient for them. To our surprise, most of them elected to stay with us.

Our neighbours in Calapandayan reacted far less favourably than the people of Pamatawan to our presence among them, partly because they felt intimidated by the ex-prisoners, but equally because they knew we were 'born again'. There was beginning to be something of a revival throughout the country in the Protestant denominations and the number of conversions was perceived as a threat by the Roman Catholic Church. Its leader in the Philippines, Cardinal Sin, had recently been conducting a vigorous campaign against the 'Born Agains', with the result that our neighbours viewed being born again not as a life-changing experience of the Lord Jesus Christ, but as a new religion hostile to their own beliefs. We could only pray that in time we would overcome their suspicion and mistrust by love.

After a year of incident and upheaval, both physical and emotional, I was becoming acutely aware of an aching sense of loneliness at the centre of my outwardly busy life. My work in the jails and at the rehab was as fulfilling as ever and it was thrilling to see my vision becoming reality, but though I knew I was liked and respected by those around me I now had no close friend in whom to confide. Dondie was the only one to whom I could talk easily and even with him my relationship was of course complicated by the fact that my dilemma concerning Stuart was still unresolved. Though he never pressed the issue, Dondie had made it plain that he wanted to marry me, while I remained as confused as ever as to the Lord's will. Then came the event which precipitated the breaking of the deadlock.

At about 4 o'clock one morning I was jerked out of sleep by the terrifying realisation that someone had crept under the mosquito net and climbed onto my bed, and as I instinctively opened my mouth to scream, a rough hand covered my mouth. It was Freddie. I tried frantically to push him away, but though small he was very strong – far too strong for me. Joy, who shared my room, slept on oblivious while I kicked and struggled in mounting panic for what seemed like hours, feeling as if I were pinned down by a wild animal under the trap of the mosquito net. Finally, in an effort to pull me closer, Freddie relaxed his hand from my mouth and I let out a piercing scream which brought the rest of the household running. Freddie leapt for the door but was seized by Dondie and the other lads and thrown out of the house.

Really it was all over very quickly, and superficially no great harm had come to me. But for many days I was gripped by fear, which gave Satan a foothold in my life and he tormented me with thoughts of what might have happened if I hadn't been able to scream. At other times, I gave way to the temptation to indulge in self-pity. How could Freddie treat me like that after all I'd done for him? I'd given him a home, a job, even the clothes on his back and he repaid me by trying to rape me.

I became withdrawn and irrational, afraid to go out alone and subject to sudden attacks of claustrophobia as the memory of being trapped under the mosquito net swept over me. Then I grew angry. I had given up so much to come here, and this was my reward. I'd be better off going home than wasting my time on people like this. Mentally I began to plan how I would return to England and find someone to replace me. But at this point Satan overplayed his hand.

'So you're giving up and going home. It was all too much for you, was it?'

I woke up to the fact that through anger and self-pity I had almost fallen for Satan's tricks. What would please him better than for me to give up? I felt faith begin to rise again, and the assurance that it would be Satan, not I, who would be defeated. In God's hands, the snare which Satan set became the means to bring me to a place of victory. My fears fell away and I was ready again for the front line.

Freddie returned to ask my forgiveness and for permission to re-enter the rehab. Though no longer afraid of him, I really didn't like the idea of living in close proximity to a man who had tried to rape me, but I knew I couldn't go on preaching forgiveness if I didn't practise it. Freddie was allowed back, but I made it clear that my forgiveness was not to be taken as condoning his behaviour. I warned him that if ever he was seen alone in a bedroom with a woman or a child, I would personally ensure that he went to jail. The safety of the other residents, especially the children, could not be put at risk on his account.

Perhaps the discovery that there was a hitherto unsuspected stern side to my nature struck him as a challenge. Not many days later, he deliberately locked himself in a bedroom with one of the children, a girl of seven. He didn't harm her and she wasn't even frightened, but the running of the rehab depended on all the residents, not just Freddie, understanding that I didn't make idle threats.

The hostility of the Subic police following my involvement in Danny's case had evaporated by now, and as I was back on friendly terms with Lieutenant Santos I went directly to the Municipal Hall to ask for his co-operation. I didn't intend to press charges against Freddie, I explained, but he needed to be taught that he couldn't flout the rules with impunity. Lieutenant Santos thought for a while and then asked, 'Does he have any tattoos? Most prisoners tattoo themselves in jail, to show which gang they belong to. These gangs are actually illegal and he could be held for a few weeks without an arrest warrant.'

So the police came and took Freddie away. We visited him and took him food while he was in jail, but when he was released I refused to have him back. There were no more chances, I told him. The children's welfare came first.

With Freddie gone, the whole episode was closed, but what remained when I reflected on it was a deep sense of thankfulness for God's protection. Dazed and half asleep, I could easily have been overpowered by Freddie's greater strength, yet the Lord had not allowed it. 'I am with you always,' said Jesus (Mt 28:20). With David, I could reply,

'I trust in You, O Lord; I say "You are my God." My times are in Your hand' (Ps 31:14–15).

The incident also forced me to ask myself how I would have coped if I'd been married to Stuart when it happened. Under the arrangement he'd proposed, I'd be here in the Philippines and he'd be thousands of miles away in England. I had no phone (even if I had, overseas calls were virtually unobtainable) and it would take a month to get a reply to a letter, which would be no substitute for the immediate comfort and reassurance I needed. Though I might never face another rape attempt, ministry to ex-prisoners would always be fraught with difficulties and disappointments. Could a marriage work if my husband were not there to share my concerns and support me through crises? The longer I thought about it, the more unrealistic it looked and the more I felt the need to know the Lord's will before embarking on marriage. One thing was already clear, however: as things stood, it would be wrong for me to commit myself to an engagement.

So when I returned to England on furlough shortly afterwards in May 1987, I gave Stuart back the ring I'd never worn. It was a beautiful ring; as beautiful as the dream it represented was unreal.

After visiting various churches in England to talk about the Philippine Outreach Centre, I'd be spending a month that summer in the United States. A missionary friend I'd met while living with Dorothy and Linda had offered to arrange a speaking engagement at a Fourth of July convention at Pinecrest Bible Institute in Syracuse, New York, and a friend of Dad's was organising an itinerary for the rest of my stay. I knew practically nothing about the people and places I was to visit, which was a sufficiently daunting prospect in itself, but just a few days before my flight to New York I received letters from several of the people Dad's friend had contacted, all regretting that it would not be convenient for me to visit.

That left just two, in Pennsylvania, plus the Bible Institute in Syracuse. At the thought of spending a whole month in the States with only three engagements I almost called the trip off, but somehow I felt that the Lord had a purpose for me in going.

With so few definite plans and very little money in my pocket, I wasn't in the best of spirits when I arrived, late in the evening, at Kennedy Airport, and though I wasn't exactly expecting to be greeted with banners and garlands of flowers, my heart sank still further when I realised that there was absolutely no one there to meet me. An awful possibility began to form in my mind, and a phone call to Pinecrest confirmed it: they weren't expecting me at all. The principal's son, who took my call, told me that my missionary friend had failed to tie up the details of my visit. The young man was very sympathetic and assured me that I would be welcome to attend the convention anyway. I'd have to fly the 200 or so miles to Syracuse, and when I checked the next flight I could afford, I found it didn't leave till the next morning. The principal's son agreed to meet me at Syracuse the following day.

I sighed as I put the phone down. Even for me, whose travels seemed never to be unattended by some such complication as overweight luggage or a lost passport, this trip looked like providing more than the usual quota of problems. I couldn't afford a hotel, so I spent the night in a chair at the airport.

When I finally arrived at Pinecrest everyone was very kind, but there was a look in their eyes that over the years I'd learned to recognise – a sort of who's-this-little-girl look, which by now no longer intimidated me. Just as well, as it turned out. Pinecrest's arrangements for the Saturday night service had fallen through and there was no speaker, so the principal, Wade Taylor, invited me to speak. 'My times are in your hand, Lord,' I thought.

In many ways it was the most imposing audience I'd ever addressed: students, graduates, pastors and academics, many of them authors of recognised works of theology. I couldn't help noticing that their average height was six feet to my five foot one. As I faced them, I felt as Peter must have felt when he took his eyes off Jesus and began to sink into the stormy sea. But the Lord responded to my cry for help and his anointing enabled me to deliver my talk with confidence and conviction. I spoke of the need to advance into the enemy's territory to take back that which belonged to the Lord, instead of being always on the defensive. The Holy Spirit moved in power that night and I believe many were challenged.

I still treasure the memory of my stay at Pinecrest. There were further opportunities to speak and profitable times of fellowship with others attending the convention – among them people working with Teen Challenge or in the New York Bronx. I got to know some of the students too, and one of them, Renee, was to become a close friend. When she discovered that my two other remaining engagements were in Allentown and Bethlehem, Pennsylvania, near to her own home town, she insisted on asking Wade Taylor for time off from her studies in order to take me there. This was an enormous relief, as I'd discovered that there were no buses to either town and I had no idea how I was going to make the 200-mile journey.

One memory stands out from all the rest. Alone in my bedroom, I heard the Lord speak to me; just four words in a still, small voice: 'Dondie is the one.'

I waited for more. I wanted it all explained, and to know exactly why Dondie was the one and Stuart wasn't. I wanted a sign, something more dramatic, to confirm what would after all be one of the most important decisions I'd ever make. 'Is that all, Lord? Do you want me to marry Dondie on the strength of "Dondie is the one"?'

There was no more, just a deep silence, impenetrable yet not empty, as if he were saying, 'It's enough. I've told you what you wanted to know.'

I'd had ample proof in recent months that I could

entrust myself to him. Yes, it was enough. My times – past, present and future – were in his hands. For the first time in over a year I had peace in my heart about my future, and I knew that Dondie really was the one. I'd never before had the confidence to say to anyone that I felt sure about whom I would marry, but next morning I told Renee that Dondie was God's man for me.

Then I wrote to Dondie.

14

The Family Band

I told my parents when I returned to England at the end of what proved to be a busy time of ministry in the States. Renee's parents welcomed me into their home and treated me as one of the family and God opened many doors for me so that I had on average a speaking engagement every other day. The rest of my trip flew past.

Mum and Dad greeted the news of my impending engagement with dismay. For one thing, they had never even met Dondie, and for another, our marriage would rule out any possibility of my ever returning to live in England. It had been hard enough for them to lose me to the mission field for an indefinite term, but this would be final. I could only hope that some of their fears would be allayed once they knew Dondie, and we arranged that they should fly out for a visit the following January. Only Nanna Jean, of the whole family, had no misgivings.

Dondie and I realised that we would be able to do little from the Philippines by way of preparation for the wedding, so we'd agreed that I should do whatever I could while I was still in England. One day while I was shopping in Manchester with Nanna, we found the perfect wedding dress. The pale pink embroidery round the bottom of the wide, hooped skirt of white taffeta lent a Filipino air to the otherwise conventional English design, as did the short puffed sleeves, which were characteristic of Filipino formal dress. Dad, summoned from his office by a hasty phone call, agreed to buy it, though with some reluctance. He saw no need to rush things. There was a whole year before the wedding, in which he secretly hoped I might change my mind.

I returned to the Philippines in September 1987, and a month later Dondie and I were officially engaged.

Renovation of the new rehab was still incomplete, though of course it was habitable by now. At the beginning of December, when we'd been there almost a year, Ronnie Castillo, our carpenter, had a surprise visitor – his brother, Alex, who had been involved in the same murder charge of which Ronnie had been acquitted. Alex and Ronnie, along with several others, had been swindled out of thousands of pesos by a man who claimed to represent a recruitment agency finding jobs overseas for Filipino workers. Having accepted their placement fees, he absconded with the money. His victims tracked him down and in the ensuing fight the man was killed.

Ronnie was delighted when Alex told him he had just been released from jail in Manila and was hoping to stay a while with his brother. When he'd been with us a few days, Alex asked us if he, his wife Marie and their family could move into the rehab on a more permanent basis, and after interviewing him I agreed. It was only then that I found out that he had five children and stepchildren and was also supporting his sister-in-law, Norma, as well as one of his nephews. However, we had room for them all now, and we soon had reason to be glad we'd accepted them. Ronnie had already become a Christian since entering the rehab and now Alex too accepted the Lord as his Saviour.

A few days later, the peace of the rehab was shattered in the dark early hours of the morning by the sound of a jeep roaring up to the entrance. It was the Subic police, come to arrest Alex who, they said, had not been released at all, but had escaped before his case had been processed. Guessing that he would seek out his brother, they had traced him to the rehab. Ronnie was arrested too for aiding and hiding an escapee.

When I visited them in the cells at the police station, Ronnie assured me he had known nothing of Alex's escape, and I believed him. I would do my best, I promised, to get him released. First of all, though, I apologised to Lieutenant Santos for neglecting to check Alex's release papers, something I did routinely with the inmates I knew personally. This was the first time, I explained, that we'd accepted a prisoner from outside the scope of our own ministry.

The officer from Manila who had come to collect Alex turned out to be a Christian and when he learned that Alex was now a believer, he promised to do what he could to get his case finished. It would be in his favour that he hadn't resisted arrest and had been found in a Christian rehabilitation home to which he'd admitted himself voluntarily. When Alex had been taken away, I managed to prevail upon Lieutenant Santos to release Ronnie.

Alex's family decided to remain in the rehab to await the outcome of his case and at every prayer meeting we prayed that the family would be reunited in time for Christmas. Christmas was very close when, one evening as we were praying, we heard noises outside, followed by Marie's loud cry of delight: it was Alex, furnished this time with the release papers that showed he had been acquitted. The anxious weeks of waiting for his case to come up had taught him something of what it means to trust the Lord, and from that time on we began to see a marked change in his character.

It wasn't long before we collected another Castillo. Jim, also an ex-prisoner, arrived at the rehab and asked to join us. He stayed for several months, but unlike his brothers he made no profession of faith in Christ. He made an effort to fit in with our way of life, but it was obviously a struggle, and one which was doomed to failure. There came a night when Alex, incensed by the fact that Jim had made a pass at one of the married women in the rehab, took him to task and their subsequent quarrel erupted into a fight in which Alex cut himself quite badly on a piece of broken glass.

It was a hair-raising scene. There was blood everywhere, Jim was hurling threats and foul language in all directions and most of the rehab members, especially the children, were terrified. My own feelings were of anger rather than fear – anger that Jim should use such words in the home we'd dedicated to the Lord. I ordered him to curb his bad language and leave the rehab for good. I had no scruples about doing this; I knew that his behaviour was not a momentary lapse but an expression of his unregenerate nature. He'd had many opportunities to put his life right with God, but he had taken none of them and clearly had no intention of doing so. In the end he left quietly, and peace was restored.

While Jim was one of our failures, Rhey was a continuing source of encouragement. Spiritually, he'd been going from strength to strength and now felt that he and Ning were ready to stand on their own feet. When they asked permission to leave the rehab, we willingly granted it and gave them some materials to build their own home. Their places were soon filled by Helen Gerez and her four small daughters. Helen, pregnant with her fifth child, had been abandoned for the second time by her ex-prisoner husband, a man I'd known for several years. Their house had recently burned down and Helen had borrowed money from a friend to build another. Since she couldn't afford a proper building plot, the new house was situated by the side of the river and was a rickety-looking structure perched precariously on stilts.

When I visited there for the first time I saw no sign of Helen, only two-year-old Clara, with a runny nose, dirty face and uncombed hair, climbing up the flimsy steps to reach the house. I learned from the neighbours that Helen went out to work at six each morning in order to pay off her loan. Before she left she would prepare breakfast and lunch for the four girls, returning at six in the evening. The three older girls were at school for most of the day, but Clara, who was supposed to be in the care of a neighbour, was often left to wander around unsupervised. My heart went out to the grubby little girl, and to poor Helen. How on earth was she going to manage with another baby? Inviting them to join us was the only solution. They moved in shortly after Rhey and his family moved out. Breathing space was never a notable feature of life at the rehab.

However, much of this was still in the future when Mum and Dad arrived just before New Year's day. Dad could only stay for three weeks, but Mum would be with us till the end of February. I had given a good deal of thought to where they should stay, especially on Dad's account. Mum had been to Subic before and I knew she'd be better at coping with the living conditions, but it was Dad's first visit and I didn't want it to be his last. Neither my own house nor the rehab offered much by way of comfort, and for someone like Dad, who wilted in the heat, the lack of air-conditioning would be a big problem. At least for the duration of Dad's stay, I persuaded them to book into the White Rock Hotel in Subic. I chose it simply because it was the best hotel in the area, often used by the US military to accommodate their visitors and new arrivals, and I had no inkling that my choice would have far-reaching consequences for the Philippine Outreach Centre.

Greatly to my relief, Mum and Dad got on well with Dondie from the start, and as they grew to know him better many of their doubts about our marriage faded, though naturally it would still be hard for them to have me based permanently in the Philippines. They joined us every day in our children's outreaches or visits to the jails and the schools, and then returned to the hotel where they had their evening meal in the restaurant. I joined them most evenings, so it was like a holiday for me too.

As is common in the Philippines, there were always live

entertainers in the restaurant and we noticed that one of the regular groups, The Family Band, sometimes included gospel songs in their performance. This wasn't really so surprising, as the hotel proprietor, Veronica Lorenzana ('Sister Onie'), whom I knew slightly, was a Christian and Pastor of the White Stone Christian Fellowship in Olongapo. The Family Band consisted of two men and three women. One of the men was obviously the father, so we guessed that one of the women must be his wife, though they actually looked more like three sisters. We invited them to join us in one of their breaks and Romy Del Monte introduced us to his wife Lourdes, his son Luis and his two daughters Roselyn and Jane, young women in their early twenties.

They were all Christians and were living in Olongapo at the time we met them, though Romy and Lourdes, full-time professional entertainers who had already worked abroad in Japan and Vietnam, were hoping for more opportunities to travel. Roselyn's dream was to be a dentist. She was singing with her parents to earn the money she needed in order to complete her training.

During their three weeks at the White Rock, Mum and Dad became quite friendly with the Del Montes, and Mum invited them to lead a praise evening at our church. When they arrived we discovered that Romy and Lourdes had seven children, all of whom, right down to the three-year-old, took part in the singing. I was irresistibly reminded of the Von Trapp family in *The Sound of Music*.

We'd been working hard on one of the rooms at the rehab and by the time Dad left I was satisfied that Mum would be comfortable in it. It had a polished floor, some decent second-hand furniture and, unlike my house, it was screened against insects. I moved in with her and we shared the room for the rest of her stay, while Joy found a new room-mate in Leonalyn, a young girl we'd taken in at the request of her father who was a prisoner at Camp Maquinaya.

Over the next few weeks, Mum, Dondie and I saw a lot of Romy and Lourdes. They accepted an invitation to sing for the inmates at Iba Jail and took to the work so naturally it was hard to believe they'd never visited a prison before. The ease with which we all worked together, and their obvious delight in this new opportunity to serve the Lord, prompted us to ask them to consider whether God might be leading them to join the staff of the Philippine Outreach Centre.

While we waited for their decision, it struck me that if they accepted it would make life easier if they lived nearer to the rehab. Besides, their house in Olongapo was by the river and subject to flooding in the rainy season, while my own house, since I'd moved in with Mum, was lying empty. Mr Cruz, his goodwill apparently not yet exhausted, readily acceded to my request for the continued use of the house to accommodate Philippine Outreach staff.

Romy and Lourdes decided to join us. They would continue with their work at the White Rock, but since this was always in the evening they would be free during the day to use their talent to serve the Lord. Within a few short weeks, the whole family of nine moved into their new home.

Then it was Roselyn's turn. 'Sister Chrissy,' she said, simply, 'I want to help with the Philippine Outreach too. What do you need?'

'Well,' I replied, 'since you ask, we really need a teacher so that we can start a kindergarten here in the rehab.'

Mum and I had been concerned for some time about the small children in the rehab who were not attending school. Marie and Alex's children, for example, having recently moved from Manila, were not eligible to enrol until the beginning of the next school year, and there were others similarly placed. At the moment, they tended to spend their day roaming aimlessly around, whereas if we could start a school, or at least a kindergarten, they would be usefully occupied and could begin to develop their learning skills. It had remained just an idea, because we had no one who could teach them.

Roselyn went away to pray and returned a few days later to say that she felt she should make herself available to teach in the kindergarten. I had to tell her that while we would do our best to support her financially, it wouldn't be a large amount. 'Actually, Sister Chrissy, I'm not looking for a salary, but if I did have some support I could enrol at night school for an education course. That way I'd be properly qualified to teach.'

Just like that, she gave up her cherished ambition to be a dentist in order to serve the Lord.

Several women in the church volunteered to help Roselyn with the teaching and what she learned at night school she planned to pass on to her fellow teachers. Between them they began to devise a curriculum, to be taught in both English and Tagalog, though of course at the point of entry the children would not yet know any English. Lessons were to take place in the rehab, in the room we used for our church services. We also planned to provide a uniform for every child, made from a big roll of yellow material donated by my generous friends on the naval base, and Mum was kept busy at the sewing machine right up to the end of her stay.

The original intention of the kindergarten was to cater for our own children, but as we made our plans I began to feel that we couldn't ignore the needs of the children in our neighbourhood. There were many poor families who couldn't afford to send their children to school and others still more needy – the children of prostitutes and pimps who were being brought up in the bars where their parents worked. We all agreed that we should open up the kindergarten to them free of charge.

However, despite the fact that there was no free education in the Philippines at that time (though things are changing now under President Ramos), many people still harboured feelings of antagonism towards us and were reluctant to entrust their children to the dubious 'Born Agains'. As a result, at our first enrolment we had only twenty pupils altogether. We received little by way of thanks at first from those who did send their children, but in time we became aware that local opinion was softening somewhat, with even the first faint signs of approval here and there.

The Del Montes became an indispensable part of the team. Romy and Lourdes soon abandoned any idea of renewing their contract abroad and threw themselves full time into the prison ministry and the work of the church. Roselyn, of course, was the lynchpin of the kindergarten and Jane, when she discovered that the burden of clerical work was becoming an increasing worry, made herself available and enrolled at college on a secretarial course. Both girls offered themselves as interpreters for me in the children's outreaches when, shortly afterwards, Joy had to leave us.

They are all just as active in the work to this day and we continue to thank the Lord for that apparently chance encounter with The Family Band.

15

Wedding Plans

Mum wanted to have a serious talk with me before she went home. She liked Dondie, but to her mind he and I were nothing like as affectionate towards each other as an engaged couple ought to be and she was worried that something was seriously wrong between us. Hurriedly I began to formulate an explanation of the strict rules of conduct which governed relations between the sexes in the Philippines, but I couldn't carry it off and instead I burst into tears and confessed to Mum that I was worried too.

The cultural differences were very real. In provincial areas particularly, any open display of affection, especially between unmarried couples, was heavily frowned on. I'd even heard of men being forced into marriage by a girl's parents just because the couple had held hands in public. Dondie and I, as Christians with pastoral responsibilities, could easily create stumbling-blocks for others if we offended against the traditional code.

I understood this intellectually, but emotionally it was a different matter. I'd been brought up in a different culture and the need for so much discretion was hard to take. Until our engagement was official, Dondie wouldn't even introduce me to his mother because to her this would in itself be tantamount to announcing our marriage; whereas in England, new boyfriends had taken me to meet their families at the earliest opportunity.

Being officially engaged didn't appear to make much difference. Surely it was natural, especially after we'd waited so long for things to come right for us, to expect Dondie to be eager to demonstrate his love for me and let the whole world see how proud he was of me? I so much wanted him to acknowledge our relationship by taking my hand, paying me compliments or singling me out with a look or a smile that was just for me. When instead he treated me just as if there were nothing special between us I felt rejected and insecure. I couldn't suppress the fear that cultural convention was only an excuse and that really he was ashamed to be seen holding hands with an English woman – or, even worse, that his feelings for me had changed.

When we were alone, which wasn't often, I taxed him with this and he would always deny it and do his best to reassure me of his love. But he wouldn't give ground over the need to abide by the restrictions imposed by the culture, while I, longing for tangible evidence of his love, continued to chafe under them.

I tried to convince Mum that Dondie and I could learn to adjust to these cultural differences, but I'm sure she realised I was trying to convince myself as much as her.

In fact, culture was not really the only factor in my unhappiness. I was also up against the fact that Dondie by nature was not given to extravagant expressions of his feelings or the sort of romantic gestures that I'd been used to from Stuart, and after Mum had left I began increasingly to compare the two of them. I remembered how good Stuart had been at creating an intimate world of romance in which 'our restaurant' and 'our song' had private significance, and a pebble picked up from the beach became a reminder of a special day. He'd plan surprises, and when he took me out to dinner or the theatre he always succeeded in making me feel like a fairy-tale princess. I didn't expect Dondie to shower me with expensive presents and outings, but I did long for little tokens such as a note or a secret smile.

I realised I was being unreasonable. Dondie was not Stuart, he was an individual in his own right with a personality of his own, and comparisons were not helpful. It was pointless to go on hankering for a fairy tale that had no basis in reality. And I couldn't doubt that God had spoken to me that night at Pinecrest.

Our wedding was set for 17th July, and in May I flew to England a month or so ahead of Dondie to finalise the arrangements. At the airport, my face was blotched with tears at the thought of leaving him for over a month, but he had his emotions well under control and while I wanted to delay the moment of parting as long as possible he seemed anxious to push me off to the departure area and get it over with. Fresh doubts assailed me and in this mood I set off to make plans for my wedding.

The dress I'd chosen a year ago was all ready apart from the final fitting, but there were plenty of other things to do. I tackled the preparations with a heavy heart, though remaining outwardly cheerful. David Chaudhary was to take the service, and David Greenow, founder of IGO, and his wife Emily agreed to stand in for Dondie's parents, as his widowed mother was much too frail to make the journey. Renee, my friend from Pinecrest, was coming over from the States to be my chief bridesmaid. Invitations were ordered, the reception was booked and everything was ready. Except me.

The nearer the wedding approached, the more my doubts increased. I loved Dondie, but if he wouldn't, or couldn't, show affection before we were married, how could I be sure it would be different afterwards? In addition, the problem of living in an alien culture took on a new and frightening aspect. After five years in the Philippines I thought I'd adjusted pretty well, but I was now face to face with the fact that the adjustment was going to be permanent. The Philippines would be my home for the rest of my life. My children would be born and brought up there, thousands of miles from the rest of my family and in conditions far removed from the comforts and conveniences of the western lifestyle I'd known as a child. As a young woman I'd dreamed of sharing a beautiful house with my husband and children, of staying home and baking bread, inviting friends for dinner, going abroad for summer holidays. Now none of this was going to happen.

One day, when I'd been in England for about a week, I walked into town and bumped into Stuart. We stood talking about this and that and after a few minutes he said, 'How about a cup of coffee for old times' sake?'

'OK, why not? It will be our last opportunity!'

In the restaurant we chatted easily. Even after two broken engagements we still got on well and enjoyed each other's company, and as we lingered over the empty coffee cups I found myself fighting to repress a feeling of regret for what might have been.

'After all we've been through,' Stuart said, 'it seems a shame that we aren't going to end up together. It would have made a great novel, like *Love Story* or something.'

In my present state of emotional confusion, this wasn't a line of conversation I wanted to pursue, so I said firmly, 'I'm sorry. Letting go of you is a sacrifice for me, but the Lord is demanding it of me.' The memory of Pinecrest was as vivid as ever.

But the effect of my words on Stuart was the opposite of what I'd intended. I could almost see the thought forming in his mind and a glimmer of hope flickered over his face.

'Maybe it's like Abraham – when the Lord sees that you're willing to give me up, then he'll allow you to marry me, just as he allowed Abraham to keep Isaac.'

I didn't answer, but later, on my own, I started to wonder. Was he right? Was it like Abraham? Would the Lord let me marry Stuart after all? I'd thought everything would be plain sailing once the Lord told me who I was to marry, but I should have known Satan better than to imagine he would leave me alone. My fears and confusion, coupled with the unsatisfactory parting from Dondie, made me vulnerable to his schemes to lure me from God's purposes.

I passed from wondering whether Stuart was right to hoping that he was. I began daydreaming once more about having a home in England and just visiting the Philippines from time to time. I played over in my mind the memories of romantic walks and candlelit dinners with Stuart. 'Lord, is it so wrong to want this?' But God seemed far away and never answered.

It was no longer possible to keep my thoughts from my parents, and Dad's reaction was decisive: 'Chrissy, you can't marry Dondie if you feel like this about another man.'

'But what about the Lord speaking to me?'

'Well, if you're feeling the way you do, you must have misheard! There's no way I can allow you to get married when you're as uncertain as this. The wedding is off. Marriage isn't a sacrifice.'

I knew that. The sacrifice demanded of me consisted not in marrying Dondie but in letting go of Stuart, and all the dreams he represented. If God said, 'Dondie is the one,' I had to accept that he knew where my true happiness lay. And whatever Dad said, I knew I hadn't misheard. 'The sheep follow him, for they know his voice' (Jn 10:4). The question was whether, having heard, I was going to follow him or my feelings.

However, Dad was right about one thing: the wedding couldn't go ahead with me in my present state. I wrote to Dondie, explaining the situation and telling him the wedding was off. Since his flight was already booked and paid for, I left it to him to decide whether he wanted to make the trip anyway. I hardly knew myself what I wanted him to do. If he didn't come, it would surely be because he accepted that our engagement was over and I'd be free to marry Stuart. Another part of me, however, clung to the conviction that once I saw him again, everything would fall back into place and I'd regain the assurance that it was right to marry him.

While I waited for his reply, I continued to waver. Stuart and I even met to fast and pray, to see if the Lord would speak again.

'It's going to be OK. The Lord is for us,' said Stuart.

'It's not,' I wept. 'God hasn't changed his mind.'

It would have been easy to pretend that he had. So many of the people at church now thought Stuart and I were ideally suited and were strongly in favour of our getting married. Mum and Dad would have been glad to be able to keep me in England. I would have had everyone's approval except God's. Since he hadn't changed his mind, I asked the Lord to confirm the word he'd spoken at Pinecrest. He didn't reply, but his silence seemed to rebuke me: 'Chrissy, I've already told you. I won't repeat myself. You choose to trust me and obey, or not.'

It was a shock when I received Dondie's reply – 'Yes, I will arrive in England as scheduled' – but also a relief. Without him I felt I would probably give way to my feelings and marry Stuart. A day or two before Dondie arrived, I went to a crusade meeting in Warrington where, with uncanny accuracy, the speaker analysed my dilemma as if he knew every detail of my circumstances. His sermon about obeying the voice of the Lord spelled out in letters a mile high that my struggle was not to do with receiving direction from God, but with being willing to walk in it.

If he was asking me to give up my dreams, I knew my God well enough to know that what he had for me was even better. '"For I know the plans I have for you," declares the Lord, "plans to prosper you and not to harm you, plans to give you hope and a future"' (Jer 29:11, NIV). I'd known it all along; it was just the old problem of translating knowledge into action and ending the emotional upheaval that was hurting not only me but

Stuart too, and all of my family. Life at home had been strained and difficult for weeks, and it was this atmosphere which greeted Dondie when he arrived, just a month before we'd been due to be married.

Imagine my dismay when it emerged that he hadn't understood the situation at all. Thinking that the wedding was merely postponed, though without any idea as to why, he had decided to make the trip as planned. Had he realised the truth, he would definitely have cancelled it. I expected him to be furious. To a Filipino, a broken engagement constitutes a huge scandal and he would have had every reason to feel that I'd humiliated him. But once the first shock was over, he amazed me by the quiet way in which he reacted. He, who of all of us had perhaps the most cause to be upset, was in fact the least perturbed.

In the following weeks, though he was actually staying with my brother, he spent most of his time with us at my parents' home, which wasn't easy for him or them. Mum especially was inclined to question him closely, because of the doubts she'd had about his love for me. But he made no attempt to ingratiate himself or plead his cause, nor did he in any way seek to put pressure on me. 'If it's God's will, it will happen,' was his only comment. Clearly he wasn't enjoying the uncertainty, but he never tried to turn the situation into a competition between himself and Stuart. When the two of them met, as they inevitably did at church, he gave no sign of being troubled at the thought of a rival, though he couldn't help but be aware that, materially at least, Stuart had so much more to offer me. Being only human I'm sure he struggled inwardly, but he never let me see it. I was baffled by his calmness; it was as if he had a secret source of tranquillity.

Though he hadn't set out to impress, his demeanour couldn't fail to have an effect on my family. It revealed more about his character than they would have learned in years under normal circumstances. A change came over me too. His refusal to try to win me by persuasion, leaving me instead to seek the Lord for myself, confirmed that he truly was the one for me, and suddenly I was able to let go of Stuart. Immediately, my love for Dondie, so long obscured, shone out again and all my doubts about his love for me disappeared. When I was eventually able to tell him that my fears and confusion had vanished, and that the Lord's will was now also my own, there was of course, Dondie being Dondie, no great explosion of delight. His smile seemed to say that he had known all along that I would reach this point.

Our only disappointment now was that the trial we'd been through had robbed us of the wedding which was due to have taken place in just a few days' time. Now that the battle was over it was hard to face the prospect of delay, but once we went back to the Philippines it would be a year or more before we could return. Here we were, with a pile of invitations and orders of service, the bride's and bridesmaids' dresses all ready and waiting – but no wedding.

After talking it over, Dondie and I decided to take Mum and Dad out for a meal and ask whether they would agree to our getting married before we went back. The chances of persuading them were admittedly slim because though they had been impressed by Dondie they still thought highly of Stuart and knew how much he wanted to marry me. Barring a miracle, they would be sure to insist that we wait at least a year.

At the end of the meal, we put our proposal and prepared to be cross-questioned, but the expected interrogation failed to materialise. Instead, they approved our plan without argument – a bigger miracle than any we had dared hope for. The date was fixed for 21st August, a Sunday.

We chose to be married on Sunday as a way of dedicating the whole occasion to the Lord, but it turned out to be a tremendous practical advantage in that booking a reception, cars and a photographer would probably have been impossible at such short notice for a Saturday. This time round I could thoroughly enjoy the whirl of preparation, but the moment which set the seal on my joy came when Dondie finally told me his side of the story.

When he first became attracted to me he hesitated to speak because of the many obstacles he foresaw to our relationship. Having spent several years in America, where two of his sisters had settled, he was only too aware of the high expectations of western women, and that I enjoyed a very comfortable standard of living in England. He feared too the possibility of discrimination against us as a mixed-race couple, not to mention the fundamental question of whether two strong-willed personalities could ever make a successful marriage.

While he was still debating with himself, the Lord spoke to him: 'Chrissy will be your wife, not because of your compatibility, nor because of your love for her, but because I have a mighty work for you to do together.' My letter from Pinecrest was simply a confirmation of what the Lord had already said, and it was his complete certainty as to the Lord's will which had enabled him to cope with my confusion so calmly. What thrilled me was the fact that he had never till now disclosed the source of his confidence; never sought to use it as a weapon to pressurise me into accepting him.

David Chaudhary was still available to take the ceremony and David and Emily to stand in for Dondie's parents. Even my bridesmaid Renee phoned from America to say she could make the revised date, despite the fact that her sister was to be married only a couple of days later.

After a week of chilly rain, I woke on the morning of the wedding to a sky of broken cloud and pale sunshine. We were to be married in the beautiful old church which the congregation, having long outgrown the original 'upper room', had bought and lovingly restored. When I arrived there with Dad, I half expected to find that many people had stayed away; the postponement of the wedding had generated a fair amount of controversy and I knew there had been a widespread feeling that I should have married Stuart. But when I walked down the aisle on Dad's arm, following the rest of the bridal party as a Filipino bride does, I couldn't hold back my tears. I'd never seen the church so full. They were all there to lend their support and share my perfect day.

The only thing we really lost was our honeymoon. We had just four brief days in Mum and Dad's holiday home in Wales and then we were back on the road and back to work. Our first speaking engagement as Mr and Mrs Dondie Perillo was in Northallerton Prison and then, in September, we returned to the Philippines.

A few years later, Stuart found the woman God intended for him and is now happily married too.

16

'Let Us Not Grow Weary'

On our return, Dondie and I moved into a room in the rehab and within three weeks of our arrival we had our first child. The idea of adoption had always appealed to me: even if I couldn't solve the problems of all the unloved children in the world I could at least make a big difference for one child. I'd talked it over with Dondie before we were married, but his response was negative and he felt sure he wouldn't be able to love someone else's child as he would his own. That was until he heard from his mother about Carlo.

I didn't meet Dondie's mother before we were officially engaged, but when he showed me her photograph I immediately recognised her as a member of the Assemblies of God church in Olongapo which I'd attended with Dorothy and Linda when I first came to the Philippines. Some of Dondie's relatives still lived in their home province of Bicol in the south of Luzon, while others had moved north to Olongapo to find work. His mother had recently gone back to be with her family in the south and one day during our engagement he received a letter from her with news of Carlo, his sister Carmen's son.

For a variety of reasons Carmen had been forced to leave the four-year-old boy in the care of Dondie's mother, and though Carlo was very happy with her, Dondie was troubled. 'Mum is old now, and becoming quite frail,' he said to me. 'It's not fair for a boy so young.'

'Well, why don't you write and ask your sister if he can come and stay with us? After we're married she may even agree to us adopting him.'

Dondie duly wrote to his sister and to his mother and both agreed that once we were married Carlo could come to live with us, which was how I found myself with a four-year-old son within two months of my wedding. Carlo, however, was no trouble at all and quickly adjusted to life in the rehab, where he happily shared a room with one of the other kids. He loved riding in our jeepney and having lots of toys to play with and within a couple of weeks he was calling Dondie and me Dad and Mum.

We'd been keen to adopt Carlo straight away so that by the time we had children of our own his place in the family would be securely established and the others would always know and accept him as their brother. It was as well, then, that he was able to come to us so soon because a week or so later I discovered I was pregnant. Filipinos believe in big families, but this was fast work even for them: three months married, with one four-year-old and a baby on the way!

I suffered quite badly with morning sickness and while there were many times when I'd have been glad to spend the day at home I couldn't neglect the ministry in the jails. Romy and Lourdes were faithful helpers, as was Romy's brother Bill who'd joined us as our jeepney driver, but none of them was yet ready to teach and preach. Since there was no one to take my place I had to carry on, trusting the Lord to give me the spiritual strength to do his work, regardless of what I was feeling.

One of our visits to Camp Maquinaya at this time stands out as the catalyst which triggered a further fulfil-ment of my original vision for the Philippine Outreach Centre. It was an open-air service and as Lourdes led the singing we began to praise the Lord, with Romy playing his portable organ and me on the guitar. While the men were gathering round, my eyes were drawn to the unusually large number of children present. There had always been children, of course, living with their parents in the jail as the sole alternative to starvation on the streets, yet today there seemed to be so many more – though it may well have been that this perception was due less to any actual increase in their numbers than to the fact that the Lord was bringing them to my attention.

Though I continued to sing and play, I have to confess that my mind was not on praising and worshipping the Lord, but on the needs of these children. Many were old enough to be in kindergarten, if not in school, yet instead they were locked up within the confines of the jail, living alongside the inmates, some of whom at least were guilty of murder, rape, drug abuse and drug dealing.

As I looked at them I heard the Lord speak to me: 'Chrissy, now is the time to take these children out of this place.'

'But Lord, we're not ready for them yet. We haven't the money or the staff. We haven't even enough beds or any of the other things we'll need if we're to care for them.'

'Look around you. Haven't you more to offer them than this?'

I looked, and my excuses suddenly seemed lame, though I hadn't made them in order to evade responsibility for the children. I genuinely wanted to help them, but everything I'd said about our limited facilities was true and Dondie had often warned me that we were becoming over-stretched.

People are called to work in different ways. There are some (and I fully understand their thinking) who look to the Lord first of all to provide the facilities and equipment before embarking on a ministry project, and to be honest I'd much rather have things that way. It would be so much less demanding. (Ever since we opened the first rehab in 1985 we'd had to exercise our faith each month just to be able to feed everyone.) But in my case, the call to reach out to the needy came first and I therefore had to believe that the Lord would give us the necessary means to care for them.

I looked again at the tough, hardened men, covered in tattoos, heads shaved, puffing away at their cigarettes; I pictured the cells with no beds, bedding or bathrooms; and indeed I saw that nothing could in any case be worse than this.

'OK, Lord, but you will have to work on Dondie. Now that I'm married I can't do just as I please. If Dondie will agree, then I'm willing.'

This was no small 'if', because Dondie was constitutionally opposed to starting up new ventures for which we were not properly prepared and adequately equipped, and it seemed likely that my pregnancy and the additional responsibility of looking after Carlo would make him even more reluctant. I had no great hopes of obtaining his consent when, on my return to the rehab, I described to him, exactly as I'd experienced it, how the Lord had spoken to me. He confounded all my expectations by immediately agreeing that we should take the children in, on condition that the women in the rehab would do their part in caring for them.

It wasn't difficult to secure the co-operation of Alex's wife, Marie, Ronnie's wife, Norma, Helen Gerez and the rest of the women. They were all more than willing to help, and just as excited at the prospect as I was. Romy and Lourdes promised their support, and Roselyn professed herself happy to welcome any new additions to the kindergarten.

Everything now rested with the inmates themselves and their willingness to accept our plans, and the women in particular couldn't be expected to hand over their children, even temporarily, without a lot of heartsearching. Some of the mothers were prisoners' wives who had chosen to join their husbands in the jail because they couldn't support their families alone on the outside. Others were members of the very small population of female inmates who were accommodated just outside the prison compound in a separate cell designed to hold twenty women, though the actual number never rose above ten.

I had no idea beforehand how our proposal would be received, but in fact the initial reaction of many inmates was one of delight, and the prison officers were so much in favour of it that they offered to provide an armed escort so that parents could visit the rehab before making a decision. Several mothers took advantage of the offer and I was glad of the unexpected opportunity to reassure them that they would be able to find us without difficulty when they wanted to reclaim their children.

They made a subdued and silent party as they followed us round the rehab, subjecting everything to the minutest examination in their anxiety to be sure their children would be happy. It was not an easy decision, however bad conditions were in the jail, and these mothers were intent on satisfying themselves that we measured up to the standard they had set in their minds. When we reached the schoolrooms and then the bedrooms with their double bunks and real mattresses, I noted the first hint of approval in their eyes, but still not a word escaped them and they finished the tour as silently as they'd begun.

Afterwards, over refreshments, they finally delivered their verdict. It was unanimous, and at a stroke the children's dormitory gained eight new occupants who moved in just as soon as we were able to have beds made for them. Of the eight, only three-year-old Kristy refused to settle and had to be returned to the jail. The four-year-olds, Marilyn, Jennalyn and Angelica gave no trouble, sleeping soundly, eating well and enjoying their first encounter with education every bit as much as Jon, Joey, Sherley and Jefferson.

In later years we took in other prisoners' children, very few of whom actually left us when their parents moved away, and of all of them none brought me greater joy than Eddie Lazaro's son, Carlito.

After the tragedy of Eddie's death in 1983 I always kept in contact with his mother, Grace, and many times, when I saw how she was struggling to put her daughter through college, I offered to have Carlito live with us in the rehab. Grace was a widow and supplemented the small income from her cleaning job by earning commission on the vegetables and fish she sold on behalf of various friends. She consistently refused my offers of help because as a strict Roman Catholic herself she wanted Carlito to have a Catholic education, and while I was disappointed I couldn't help but admire her determination.

She managed to pay for him to attend a private Catholic school from kindergarten through to the final year of elementary school, but at this point her financial problems became overwhelming and she was at last compelled to seek my help.

'Sister Chrissy, Carlito is supposed to graduate this month, but the sisters at the school have warned me that if I don't pay my outstanding tuition fees, he won't be able to. Sister, Carlito says he would like to live with you at the rehabilitation home and if you are willing to sponsor him at school, we'll be really grateful.'

My heart leaped. By now Carlito was, I well knew, quite a mischievous teenager, but through the years I'd treasured the hope, for Eddie's sake, of being able to do something for his son. Paying off the outstanding fees would strain our budget to the limit, but I was confident that the Lord would meet this need and (it was still my practice not to hand over cash) arranged to go with Grace to the school to settle the debt.

That done, she invited me to her home, which was now in a district of Olongapo, and reaching it, she warned me, would involve quite a hike up the hillside. As we climbed the narrow dirt track worn by the constant passage of feet – there was no proper road – I wondered what it would be like to do this in the rainy season. It was treacherously slippery even when dry, but Grace, a grandmother in her fifties, scrambled nimbly to the top without a word of complaint.

The house was perched on the hillside with three others and though it was just a *kubo* (native Filipino house) with a dirt floor, Grace was very proud of it. Carlito was waiting there for our arrival, excited as he'd always been whenever I paid them a visit, and eager to talk to me. Conversation had to wait, however, until, at Grace's insistence, he'd changed out of his school uniform and hung it neatly on a hanger. 'Laundry soap is so expensive at the *tindahan* (corner shop),' she explained, 'but in Olongapo you can get a bargain. If you buy the whole bar you get one free, so I'm avoiding using soap until I can afford the full bar. Carlito knows how to keep his uniform clean so that it doesn't have to be washed every day.'

To look at Carlito you would never have guessed that his clothes were not washed daily; he looked as well turned out as any of the children at his private school. I caught a glimpse of the extent to which careful thrift had dominated Grace's life, enabling her to survive and support her family for so many years. How many people in Britain would think twice about buying a whole bar of soap? But in the Philippines such things are an inescapable fact of daily life for many. Laundry soap is sold in long bars which can be broken into four smaller pieces and as there are so many poor people who can't afford the whole bar, the smaller shops sell each piece separately. Similarly, you can buy a single stock cube instead of a full box and items such as shampoo and toothpaste are usually sold in small sachets because a full bottle or tube is beyond the means of the poor.

Grace had not been made bitter by the relentless need for economy, and her testimony was that God had met their every need. On one occasion, with her purse empty and no food in the house, she was walking home wondering how they were to eat that night when, glancing down, she saw a 500 peso note lying at her feet. For that she gave God the glory.

So Carlito came to live with us. He remained as mischievous as ever, but I continue to rejoice that we were able to lead him to accept Jesus as his Lord and Saviour.

When the children from Camp Maquinaya joined us we had been in the new rehab for almost two years and as the slow process of renovation neared completion we began to think about an official opening. In a few months' time I was expecting a number of visitors: Jonathan and Rodney, two of our trustees, were planning to visit the Philippines with a couple of missionary friends and would be calling in on us in January; and Nick, who'd given me my first lessons in evangelism, would be in the country at the same time. Best of all, Nanna Jean would be here too. I'd never imagined that she would be able to come, as she was now in her seventies, but so great was her desire to witness at first hand the work she'd prayed for and supported for so long, that she was prepared to risk the exhausting journey in order to be with us. It seemed the ideal time for the opening and we set the date for 7th January 1989.

We sent out invitations to missionary friends and local churches, and then set about the task of making the rehab ready for public viewing. We had a lot of decorating still to do, but the most expensive remaining job was finishing the windows, which at present had screening but no glass. Daily we brought our need to the Lord at the early morning prayer meeting, and with just a few days to go before the opening his answer came in the shape of an unusually large gift from our supporters back home.

The day arrived and while I escorted our guests from England on visits to the prisons and children's outreaches, the men were busy at the rehab finishing off the painting, putting up a platform for the opening service and erecting a tent covering over it to provide shade from the scorching sun. Meanwhile, the women were cleaning and preparing food for the banquet which was to follow the service. With so many visitors expected, there were five pigs to be slaughtered, three of which were spit-roasted over an open fire in traditional Filipino celebration style.

Like a bride on her wedding day, I was in a state of happy confusion as events flashed past me at bewildering speed, and though both the service and the banquet went according to plan I have only the haziest recollection of them. So many friends were there: members of various churches in Olongapo joined with us, and Romy's other brother, who was a pastor in Olongapo, brought his entire congregation; Pop Pederson, who had replaced Pop Houghton, came from the US Military Mission; and several fellow missionaries travelled from north and south to take part in our celebration.

But the greatest blessing was that so many of our unbelieving neighbours, having steadily opposed us ever since we moved into the district, were there that day to hear the testimonies of the ex-prisoners and the preaching of God's word. We had been praying for two years that the Lord would break down the barriers, and this was just a foretaste of what was to come. No doubt the prospect of sharing the banquet had played its part in persuading them to attend, but God's word is never sent out in vain and the planted seed would one day yield a harvest if we were patient. 'Let us not grow weary while doing good,' says St Paul, 'for in due season we shall reap if we do not lose heart' (Gal 6:9).

17

The Way to Success

Damp eyed, I gazed in wonder at my beautiful newborn daughter.

Dondie hadn't been able to leave the rehab to come with me when I flew to England to have the baby, so it was Mum and not he who was at my side when Monique was born on 6th June 1989. It was hard to be away from my husband for several months after being married for less than a year, and like most women I'd wanted him to be with me when I gave birth to our first child. It was only the sight of Monique, when the nurse laid her beside me, that eventually dried the tears I hadn't been able to hold back after Mum had gone.

I'd also been hoping to introduce Carlo to his new brother or sister straight away and but for delays in the processing of his adoption papers and visa documents he would have travelled with me. As it was, he'd had to stay behind in the Philippines with Dondie and now I wouldn't see either of them until September. While it was painful to be separated from my husband and son, I resolved to make the most of the opportunity to be with my loved ones in England, whom I might not see again for some considerable time. I was beginning to realise that trips to the UK would become rarer as our family grew because of the high cost of flying.

Within a very short time of Monique's birth I was back on the road for my usual round of speaking engagements, and the long journeys were now complicated by the routine of feeding and nappy changing which dominates life with a small baby. Before I spoke I would have to disappear for a while to give her a top-up feed, and then hand her over to her nanna. It certainly wasn't easy, but it had to be done if I were to fulfil my commitment to raise support for the Philippine Outreach Centre.

Thankfully, I had a companion to help me when I flew back in September. Vanessa was twenty years old and while attending a missions weekend at Hollybush had sensed God calling her to serve him for a time in the Philippines. She talked it over with Jonathan, one of the Hollybush staff and also one of my trustees, and he, knowing we desperately needed extra help, suggested that I should meet Vanessa and the missionary director of her church in Leeds. It was obvious to me that she just wanted the Lord to use her in whichever way he chose and the church elders testified to her faithfulness and zeal for evangelism, so it was soon agreed that she should join us for a year.

Vanessa settled in without difficulty. She quickly made friends with the young people in our church and having done a college course in pre-school education she was a great help in the kindergarten, where she and Roselyn were able to pool their resources and learn from each other's experiences. All her pupils loved her, and she them. She had a great gift for relating to people naturally and easily, and struck up a particular friendship with Albert, the brother of one of our young people. Albert had Down's syndrome and though he was nineteen he had never been to school because there was no provision for special educational needs in our area at that time. He was so fond of Vanessa that when he discovered she was a teacher in the kindergarten, nothing would satisfy him but to enrol as a pupil. He rarely missed a day until he graduated and went on to the local elementary school.

The kindergarten was doing extremely well. Our neighbours had set aside much of their earlier suspicion and started to trust us not to impose some alien religion on them, with the result that more of them were sending their children to us. It was equally gratifying to hear of the favourable opinions passed by staff at the elementary school on the quality of the graduates they received from our kindergarten.

At the rehab too everything seemed to be in excellent shape, with all the current residents making steady progress; none of them missed even the 6 o'clock morning prayer meeting, though we never made it compulsory. And Joseph's progress was little short of spectacular. Soon after that inauspicious beginning, when he turned up at our prayer meeting completely drunk, he had given his heart to the Lord and the change in his life was so dramatic that we readily acceded to his request for sponsorship at Bible school.

Basking in the warmth of these successes, we were totally unprepared for the violent upheaval which shook the rehab to its foundations. It was November, and I was hard at work in the office on our preparations for Christmas, when the quiet of the afternoon was ripped apart by shrill screams and the clamour of raised voices. I rushed out, and there at the centre of the commotion was Alex's stepdaughter, Maria Castillo. I'd never seen so much blood in my life; her school uniform was absolutely soaked in it. While Bill Del Monte hurried to get the jeepney started to take her to hospital, I tried to find out what had happened.

It appeared that Maria had suddenly started to bleed internally at school and her teacher had simply told her to go home. In that condition she'd walked all the way up the hill to the rehab, alone. Maria's mother, Marie, and her aunt, Norma, came with us in the jeepney and none of us spoke during the thirty-minute ride to the General

Hospital in San Marcelino, just to the north of Castillejos. I was thinking some very unwelcome thoughts.

Maria had known plenty of unhappiness in her short life. Before they came to the rehab her mother would often keep her away from school to help with the younger children, so that at fifteen she was still at elementary level. As a small child she had lost the sight of her left eye when her younger brother poked it with a stick, and the injury had destroyed the iris, giving her a freakish appearance which made other children afraid of her. We had sought the help of a mission on the US naval base and while nothing could be done to restore her sight she'd been fitted with a contact lens which worked well cosmetically and had given her the confidence of knowing she looked normal to her classmates.

And now fresh trouble of a much worse kind had come to her. Without my asking, the Lord had shown me the truth of what had happened to Maria and the knowledge dismayed me.

The hospital at San Marcelino, though quieter and cheaper than the General Hospital in Olongapo, was no better off as far as facilities were concerned and we waited a long time before the nurses came to attend to Maria. When they did come their treatment of her was anything but sensitive. They handled her roughly and one of them demanded, 'Who's the boy?' When Maria made no reply, she repeated impatiently, 'Come on, tell us! Who's the boy? Is it someone at school?'

'No, no!'

'Well, it must be somebody. Who was it?'

It was a painful scene; poor Maria was shaking her head in distress at the nurses' accusations, while to them the suspicion that she was miscarrying as a result of sex outside of marriage rendered her an object of contempt. Instead of offering comfort, Marie also turned on her daughter: 'Maria, tell us who it was!'

This made me angry as I was sure Marie must already know. I told them all to be quiet and leave the girl alone and demanded a private interview with the female doctor in charge. 'Please don't be so hard on her,' I said when we were alone. 'It's not her fault. I know her. She comes straight home from school every day and never goes out anywhere.'

'Then why doesn't she answer us?'

'I don't know for sure yet, but I think her stepfather is the one responsible.'

'Why doesn't she say so?'

'Probably she's afraid of him. He's an ex-prisoner with a violent history and she's very likely scared of what he might do.'

Having secured a promise that Maria would be treated more gently I went back to Maria herself, and without pressing her to talk assured her that I was there for her if she needed me. Leaving Norma and Marie to look after her, I went back to the rehab.

I decided to say nothing just yet to Alex. Anything I did would have repercussions both for Maria and the other five children under his authority and my first priority was to seek the Lord for wisdom in handling the situation. I realised now why Maria's elder sister Jackie had suddenly left the rehab a year or so ago. She'd gone out one day, ostensibly to do some shopping, and never returned. Afterwards, she wrote to Dondie and me, thanking us for all we'd done for her, but she didn't give her address or explain why she had left.

When talking to us about Alex's past, though they had spoken of his violence, neither Marie nor the children had ever hinted that he'd been guilty of sexual abuse. On the evidence available to us, therefore, we'd felt we had good reason to be encouraged by the progress he'd made since he joined us. His temper still flared up at times, but such occurrences were not common and, especially at the beginning, he'd seemed to be doing well in other ways. He began to develop a gift for preaching and had even asked us to pray that the door would be opened for him to return to his home town to spread the gospel there. It was undeniable, however, that when his brother Jim came to the rehab he had influenced Alex for the worse, and because Jim refused to leave the area after he was expelled, his influence remained.

When I confided to Dondie what I believed the Lord had shown me, we decided together that we should take no action until we had spoken to Maria and ascertained what she wanted to do. One morning shortly after this, when I arrived at San Marcelino to visit Maria, I found her aunt Norma sitting by the entrance to the hospital, distraught and red eyed. Struggling to get the words out, she managed to say, 'Oh, Sister Chrissy, you'll never believe it!' before breaking down again.

I put my arm round her. 'I know already. The Lord revealed to me that Alex is to blame. Has Maria told you?'

Still sobbing, she nodded in reply as we walked towards Maria's ward. Before we went in, Norma turned to me and said, 'Please don't tell Alex or Marie that you know. Maria hasn't told her mother yet. She's so frightened of what Alex will do if he discovers we all know.'

I spent a little while with Maria and she admitted to me herself that Alex was responsible. It had all happened while I was in England following the birth of Monique, and Maria had carried the burden of her dreadful secret all alone until now. Alex had planned his assault carefully. When the rehab's pigs were close to delivering their piglets, he would take his mosquito net and sleep outside by the pigsties in order to be on hand to help them. He had lured Maria out to him by insisting that she bring his coffee and it was there, where no one would see or hear anything, that he had raped her.

While Norma comforted Maria I went again to speak to the doctor. 'If the child wants to press charges against her stepfather, we'll support her. Can I rely on you to provide proof that she was raped, or at least that she had a miscarriage?' I asked.

'I've never said she had a miscarriage.' (This was true; it had been implied but never openly stated.) 'This kind of haemorrhage sometimes does occur in teenage virgins, though we don't know the cause.'

'How can you say that? When she was first admitted you were so certain there was a boy involved, you were condemning her for it. Now that she's confessed the truth, you're denying it.' I was utterly exasperated. There could be no rape case without medical testimony. Perhaps the doctor, knowing that Alex had a violent past, refused to get involved for fear of reprisals; it was certain that the medical records didn't disclose the true facts. When I checked them they said simply: 'Normal haemorrhage in adolescent female.'

In spite of the doctor's obduracy I assured Maria that I would still support her if she wanted to go ahead and file a rape charge. But she couldn't face the prospect of confronting Alex in court, nor did she want him to find out that we knew, and as no charge could be brought without her consent I accepted her decision. However, she agreed that for the sake of her nine-year-old sister Tina, and even the baby Mary Grace, she would expose Alex if he ever tried to harm her again.

Dondie and I were in a difficult position now. We couldn't charge Alex without Maria's consent, and in any case we'd given our word not to. If we confronted him ourselves he might well leave the rehab taking his family with him, and Maria's position would be worse than before. There seemed no alternative but to maintain a pretence of ignorance while we prayed for guidance.

Two weeks after Maria was discharged from hospital, as Vanessa and I were packing Christmas stockings for the children's outreaches, the rehab once more echoed to the sound of frantic screaming. It was Maria, thrown into a panic by Alex demanding that she bring him some coffee to the pigsties. Quickly, Dondie and I locked Maria in our room with Vanessa and Monique and rushed out to look for Alex, but there was no sign of him. He knew now that his sin had been exposed.

Several hours later we were all startled by a loud bang, then another – gunfire? Christmas fireworks? – followed by the sound of Alex's drunken shouting, which terrified everyone, especially his family who knew from past experience what he was capable of when drunk. The noise was coming from the kitchen and when Dondie and I hurried over there we heard Alex's voice: 'How about you, Brother Bill? You're a man. Are you willing to fight?'

We burst in to find that Alex had Bill firmly pinioned and was pressing a wicked foot-long *bolo* (knife) against his throat. Instinct took over and I ran towards them. 'Alex, in the name of Jesus, give me that knife.' He might as well have been made of stone. 'Alex,' I repeated more urgently, 'in the name of Jesus, give it to me.'

Slowly he released his hold on Bill, who darted away and ran for safety. Alex began to wave the knife at me and Dondie. 'How about you, then, Brother Dondie?'

Dondie and I were both convinced that he was planning to kill one of us and then take his own life, and each of us called on the Holy Spirit for wisdom to prevent him. All the others had cleared the area, keeping the women and children out of danger, so we were alone. We found the strength to ignore Alex's threats and speak to him calmly, discovering true wisdom in Solomon's words: 'A soft answer turns away wrath, but a harsh word stirs up anger' (Prov 15:1). Gradually his anger subsided and he began to show signs of remorse. 'There's no hope for me now. This time I've gone too far.'

If he would repent, we told him, the Lord would be faithful and just to forgive, provided his repentance was genuine. 'How can you forgive me for this?' he asked, handing the knife to Dondie.

'Alex, our heart's desire is to see you restored to the Lord, not for you to be destroyed.'

Of course, for the children's sake we couldn't have

allowed him to stay at the rehab, but we didn't have to ask him to go. He left of his own accord immediately, quiet and broken, hanging his head. 'I've gone too far now,' he said softly.

Marie, afraid of what her husband might do, had already fled with Mary Grace and didn't come back till the next day, having spent the night in the market place. When she learned that Alex had left she decided to go after him, taking only Mary Grace and leaving the other children with us. They found a house in Pamatawan and Alex has since visited the church from time to time though as yet, like Esau, he has found no place for repentance.

Jackie and Maria are both married now with children of their own, and with the exception of one of the boys the rest of Alex's and Marie's children are still with us, including Mary Grace who returned to us a year or so after Alex left. The future looks bright for them all.

This incident was the worst we had yet encountered at the rehab. When it was over Bill Del Monte expressed his doubts to me: 'Don't you see now, Sister Chrissy, that you ought to give up with people like this? They'll never change. You're just wasting your time.'

I thought before I answered. 'Brother Bill, I'm not called to be successful and I'm not called to change these people. I know I could never change anyone. What I am called to be is obedient. We opened the rehab for people like Alex because the Lord told us to, not because we wanted to be successful and not for its sensation value. I can't stop just because of this failure.' I remembered my own failures which God had redeemed, and went on, 'I have to be obedient. If God tells us to stop, we will. What's important is our willingness to obey him.'

I can't deny that I feel disappointed when those whom I've tried so hard to instruct in the ways of God go astray. However, I always keep in the forefront of my mind a lesson which my mother taught me, gleaned from her own experience of similar disappointments with the young offenders who lived in our home. One of the boys had stolen her purse which was later found, empty, in a local pub. It had been hard enough for her to discover the theft, but to learn that he had spent the money on drink added insult to injury. She felt so let down after all she'd done for him. She told me, 'And then I cried out to the Lord. "What do I have to do for them? Do I have to die for them?"'

His reply shook her to the core: 'No, Mary. I did that.'

Without realising it, she had encroached on God's prerogative and lost sight of what was his responsibility and what was hers. Her ministry to the boys had filled her horizon to the exclusion of the need for God to act.

I learned from her mistake never to think that I have the power to change other people. I can lead them, guide them by example and treat them with love and compassion, but none of this will bring about a change in their lives. God alone can bring about that change in a man which will affect him for eternity. Man cannot even change himself by will power: '"Not by might nor by power, but by My Spirit," says the Lord of hosts' (Zech 4:6).

When there are changed lives and successes, I can't boast about them, 'for it is God who works in you both to will and to do for His good pleasure' (Phil 2:13). Equally, I can't complain about what appears to be failure; these situations too are in his hands.

What then constitutes success for a missionary, or a pastor, or any child of God? The secret of success, I believe, lies in these words:

> This Book of the Law shall not depart from your mouth, but you shall meditate in it day and night, that you may observe to do according to all that is written in it. For then you will make your way prosperous, and then you will have good success (Josh 1:8).

If by God's grace we are obedient to his word, then 'in due season we shall reap if we do not lose heart'.

18

Jimmy

Ever since I first met Mom and Pop Houghton in my early days in the Philippines I'd kept up my links with the US Military Mission's Servicemen's Home here in Subic. It was an independent mission financed for the most part by supporters in the States, with occasional additional funding from the churches inside the Olongapo naval base, where the Houghtons had numerous friends and contacts. It was through Mom and Pop that I'd had invitations to speak on the base and the Christians there had been extremely generous in their support of the Philippine Outreach Centre.

The Houghtons had been dear friends, helping and encouraging me through some of my darkest times, and I'd missed them when they returned to the States to continue their ministry with the Assemblies of God. However, it wasn't long before I became acquainted with the Pedersons who came to replace them and with their daughter and son-in-law, the Fishers. The Fishers were serving with the US military and like Dondie and me were newlyweds, with a son not much older than Monique.

When the Pedersons had to return unexpectedly to America because of illness, they entrusted the care of the Servicemen's Home to the Fishers, with whom Dondie and I became good friends. For me especially, it was a treat to spend time with people who came from a culture like my own and enjoy for a while the western comfort of the Home.

In their turn, the Fishers too needed to leave the Philippines quite suddenly and as they had no one to whom they could hand over the Servicemen's Home they turned to Dondie and me for help. Would we take over their role, just for a few months at most, until other arrangements could be made?

The suggestion was not as impossible as might first appear. For one thing, most of the work involved would be in the evenings; the purpose of the Home was to provide a drop-in centre for the men from the ships which were constantly coming and going at the base and we could expect visitors any time after 7pm. For another, the number of servicemen actually using the Home had been greatly reduced by the restrictions which sometimes placed Subic off limits to military personnel. (Ever since President Corazon Aquino defeated Ferdinand Marcos in the elections of 1986, the NPA [New People's Army], a group of Maoist insurgents whom Marcos had ruthlessly suppressed, had been threatening the US military, and a number of servicemen and some missionaries had been killed. Whenever trouble seemed imminent the military authorities would restrict the movements of their personnel and the men in our area would be confined to Olongapo.)

With this in mind, and since the job would be for only a short time, Dondie and I accepted, and in February 1990 we moved into the Home, which was just a five-minute drive from the rehab and closer to the centre of Subic. We soon fell into a routine, with Dondie spending most of the day up at the rehab while I continued as usual to visit Camp Maquinaya and Iba Jail with the Del Montes. The evenings, naturally, were spent at the Home waiting for any servicemen who might call, and if a crisis arose at the rehab during the night Bill, the jeepney driver, had instructions to come immediately to fetch us.

Some of our work for the Military Mission took us onto the base. On Friday evenings we joined a Bible study there, which gave us an opportunity to meet servicemen and invite them to the Home, and it also led to me being asked to teach once a week at a women's group. Every Wednesday we attended the chaplains' luncheon along with other military missionaries, local pastors and the military chaplaincy, and from time to time we received invitations to speak at the chapels on the base about the Servicemen's Home and the Philippine Outreach Centre.

Being responsible for two missions was hard work, but there were many compensations, of which access to certain facilities on the base was only one. Our visits to the servicemen's launderette each week after the Wednesday luncheon meant that Monique's baby clothes emerged beautifully soft from the tumble drier and we no longer used towels that felt like scrubbing brushes after being baked dry in the hot sun. And instead of taking Carlo and Monique to play on the beach, which was really none too clean, we were able to take them to McDonald's and the children's playground, treats they enjoyed enormously.

The Servicemen's Home itself, though it would have been judged ordinary by the standards of the better houses in Manila, was luxurious compared to those in Subic. It was two-storeyed and spacious, set in its own large garden, where Lora, the cook, had her own house. The lounge had a polished wooden floor and furniture (donated by a service family who'd been relocated) better than anything available in Olongapo. The small marble-tiled kitchen delighted me because in addition to a huge fridge it also contained the first oven I'd had since coming to the Philippines. An impressive wide stone stairway led to the first floor where the master bedroom boasted a king-size water bed, also the gift of a departing service couple, and, unbelievably, an en suite bathroom where the shower actually dispensed *hot* water, something unknown at the rehab. A door on the landing opened onto a large balcony directly over the lounge. Best of all, for the first time we had privacy and a place of our own as a family, so I wasn't too troubled when the months went by without any news of who was to replace us.

In the meantime, things were not standing still at the Philippine Outreach Centre while we were at the Home. John Morales, a converted ex-prisoner who had been detained at Muntinlupa and had heard of me from Mammie Olga, sought us out to ask if he could work with us in the prison ministry. He'd already gained experience by visiting the jail in his wife's home town of San Fernando and after taking him several times to Iba, where he quickly demonstrated a gift for communicating with the inmates, we gladly invited him to join us. He moved into the rehab with his wife and four children and in the year or so that they were with us, John was instrumental in expanding our work to include San Fernando Jail, about thirty miles north-east of Subic.

The church also was experiencing change. Dondie had been feeling for some time that the church's outreach would be more effective if our meeting place were nearer to the town centre than the rehab, and when he and I moved into the Servicemen's Home we noticed that a small restaurant on the same street was available for rent. It was small, but Dondie was satisfied that the location would benefit the work. He was right too, and church membership grew steadily from the time we began to meet there.

But it was meeting with Jimmy that sparked off the vision that was to live with me for the next three years. Not long after we moved to the Home I was asked by an anxious parent to visit a young man of twenty who was being detained at our local *barangay* station (a sort of small police station, but staffed by appointed civilians, where law breakers can be held until the police are informed and a formal arrest made). As the young man's offence was a minor one he would soon be released, and after speaking to him for a while I turned my attention to another detainee, wondering what on earth he could be guilty of. He looked about nine years old.

'What's your name?' I asked in Tagalog.

'Jimmy,' he replied shyly.

'And how old are you?'

'Twelve!'

'What has he done?' I asked the *barangay* captain.

'Oh, he was found roaming the streets at midnight, so he'll be kept here for three days.'

His mother, it appeared, worked in one of the nearby bars as a hostess, which was a euphemism for 'legal prostitute' (though street-walking was illegal, prostitution as a service provided in the bars was not). Jimmy's light skin and brown hair suggested that his father was a westerner, most probably an American serviceman.

I was overwhelmed with compassion for Jimmy, whose only crime was that he had no one to see that he was safely in bed at night. His mother hadn't been to see him since he was picked up, he told me, and he'd been too upset all that day to eat. Turning again to the captain, who knew of the Philippine Outreach Centre, I asked, 'Can I take him out for a while? I'll just show him round the rehabilitation home and give him something to eat, and I'll have him back within a couple of hours.'

'Sure, go ahead.'

'Jimmy, would you like to come with me?'

His little face lit up and his smile was all the answer I needed. He climbed happily into the old station wagon belonging to the Servicemen's Home and looked out of the window to see if any of his friends were around to notice him riding in a car with a white lady. To get to the rehab we had to pass the back of the bars and he pointed out to me the one where he lived with his mother and sister, at the same time waving and shouting to his friends, laughing at their wide-eyed astonishment.

At the rehab the children crowded round to be introduced to Jimmy. I took him on a tour of the building and he stared in silent delight at the kindergarten school rooms with their little red and green chairs and bright pictures, numbers and alphabets displayed on the walls. From the bedrooms, where I'm sure he could hardly believe there were such good strong bunks for all the children, we proceeded to the kitchen where he disposed of his rice and fish in record time, in spite of the attentions of the other kids who couldn't wait for him to finish so that they could show him their television.

When I asked him if he liked the rehab the answer was an emphatic 'Yes!'

'Would you like to stay here if your mum would let you?'

'Oh, yes!'

The two hours were soon up, and after I'd taken him back I decided to visit his mother. The atmosphere inside the bar was dark and close, and the dim illumination of the red light bulbs revealed hand-painted murals of half-naked women. Though the bars never actually closed, it was very quiet during the daytime. Jimmy's mother proved to be outside at the back and as I walked uneasily along an unlit corridor in search of her my feelings about her were mixed. This was no place for her to be bringing up a child; and yet I knew that many young teenagers from the provinces were sent by their families to earn money in the towns where, lacking education, they had little chance of finding a decent job and so ended up as this woman had.

When I found her she was washing clothes and instead of returning my smile she turned coldly away and went on with her work. She had already heard from her neighbours that Jimmy had been to the rehab and I could tell that she felt I was critical of her. Yet who was I to condemn her? But for the grace of God I might have found myself in the same position. I tried to convince her that what I felt was compassion, not criticism, and that I was only interested in helping her and her son. Jimmy would be welcome, I told her, to stay at the rehab if she became unable to support him; I knew that she must be earning less than usual since the restrictions kept servicemen away from the bars.

She eventually unbent a little, but she wouldn't allow Jimmy to come to us. Of course, I was disappointed. He was such a sweet little boy and I hated the thought of him living in the brothel, but even if I'd had the means I still couldn't help every child who tugged at my heartstrings. They had parents or guardians who loved them in their way and would never give them up, and now that I was a mother myself I understood this. I knew I would go to any length to prevent my children being taken away. I would scrub floors in order to feed them – anything rather than hand them over to someone else.

It was then that the Lord gave me a vision to start a school. We already had the kindergarten and it was doing very well, but at the age of seven the children had to move on to the local public elementary school, where those who had no other Christian influence in their lives would quickly forget what we had taught them about the ways of the Lord. If we had our own school they would have a Christian education from the age of three to sixteen and even if I couldn't care for all the Jimmys of Subic, some of them at least would have the chance of a better future. The rice and fish I'd given Jimmy would do him good for one day, whereas by educating a child in a good Christian school we could be instrumental in affecting both his eternal destiny and also the rest of his life on earth.

Jimmy himself moved away from the area the following year, but I would never forget him because it was through him that God gave me the vision for the Philippine Outreach Academy. I didn't know how long it would take to come to fruition and I'd learned by now that God can't be rushed. He has a perfect time for everything, and it's never early and never late.

In the meantime, however, I had to address more immediate concerns. My vision of a Christian school made me realise just how far the public school system was failing the rehab children. For one thing, because the school had no uniform they would set off each day in their flip-flops and ill-assorted clothes looking thoroughly dejected and untidy, and I was sure their lack of smartness was eroding their self-respect. They also appeared to have little enthusiasm or motivation in their work, which was hardly surprising as the teaching was erratic and they would often be sent home if the teacher was busy attending a meeting. Their academic achievement, in fact, was negligible.

Since, therefore, our own school was still in the future, I began to make enquiries about enrolling them in a private Christian school I knew of in Olongapo. White Stone Academy was run by Sister Onie, owner of the White Rock Hotel in Subic, and used an American system known as ACE (Accelerated Christian Education). I discovered, however, that to enrol our twenty children would cost far more than we could afford at present, so we all began to pray, especially the children who were very excited at the idea of going to a private school.

I was familiar with the ACE programme as my parents had once considered starting a school at the Upper Room, and I thought it would be useful for the children to follow an American curriculum because most professional jobs in the Philippines demand a good command of English. It would also be an advantage for them to have lessons conducted in English rather than Tagalog from elementary level as English was the language in which they would all be taught at high school. The ACE curriculum is divided into modules called 'paces' and there is a strong emphasis on self-directed study designed to prepare students for the sort of responsibility that will be required of them when they eventually go to college. Though a supervisor is always on hand, the children work individually, setting their own goals, checking and marking their own completed tasks and testing themselves on the contents of each pace prior to a mini-exam in which they must achieve at least ninety per cent before they can proceed to the next module. Motivation is stimulated by awarding prizes and privileges for good behaviour and academic achievement, and here in the Philippines the individual learning is supplemented by more interactive lessons in music, art and PE.

The standards reached in ACE schools were very high, even compared to other private schools, and I was satisfied that our children would benefit from the programme. The only problem (as usual!) was the cost. Even with the very generous discount which Sister Onie offered, the fees were still beyond what we could manage. On my last trip to England, Rodney, one of my trustees, had suggested starting a sponsorship programme to help with our finances, pointing out that our supporters might prefer to give to a particular person or project rather than to the Philippine Outreach in general. Though I hadn't yet followed up his suggestion, it struck me that many people might respond to a request to sponsor a child through school – if only we had time to ask them. But the time for enrolment was fast approaching and a decision had to be taken now.

After much prayer, I received the assurance that sponsors would come forward and that we should trust the Lord by enrolling the children immediately. Then the work began. Each student needed two uniforms, one for everyday and one for special occasions, which meant forty uniforms to be ordered. I got every child to trace the outline of his or her foot on a piece of paper so that I could go to Manila to buy twenty pairs of shoes, along with literally hundreds of notebooks, dozens of pencils and pencil sharpeners – the list was endless and the bills alarming. Through unexpected gifts and the support of my home church in England, God graciously provided for all these expenses and by June 1990 the children were ready for their first day at White Stone.

What a difference it was to see them setting off, excited and happy in their neat new clothes – white blouses and navy pleated skirts for the girls and short-sleeved white shirts and navy trousers for the boys. Proper shoes, too, and clean white socks. The uniforms were inspected daily at school and from taking pride in their appearance they grew in confidence and self-esteem, which spilled over into their work so that though some of them had initially been placed in a grade below the one they'd been in at the public school, they made rapid progress and soon caught up.

It had been a big step of faith when we enrolled them, but I never had cause to regret it. In addition to confirming my confidence in the ACE programme, the obvious benefit to the children gave me an added incentive to hold on to the vision God had given me and to look to the day when we could put the programme into practice in our own school. As the year went on, small groups, couples and individuals began to come forward to sponsor the children at White Stone and I believed even more strongly that the Lord would surely provide the means to make the Philippine Outreach Academy a reality.

When 1991 arrived, Dondie and I were still at the Servicemen's Home, 'a few months' having stretched to twelve, and even now there was no firm news of our successors. We began, however, to move ahead with plans to open our new school in the summer of that year. Everyone who will be responsible for running an ACE school – the principal, the pastor, the administrator and the teaching supervisor – has to undergo a short course of instruction in the implementation of the programme and in June, by which time I was three months pregnant with our second baby, we were all looking forward to our training when Pinatubo erupted and our plans, along with much else, were reduced to rubble.

19

Pinatubo

Dondie and I walked into a scene of unwonted confusion on the naval base when we arrived for the chaplains' luncheon on Wednesday 12th June. The owners of hundreds of cars, which were parked everywhere in the most unlikely places, were variously occupied in unloading their picnic baskets, walking their dogs or joining one of the long queues of people waiting to be allocated temporary accommodation.

It had been rumoured for several days that Clark Air Base in Angeles City was to be evacuated to the naval base as a safety precaution following news of the impending eruption of Mount Pinatubo, one of the more than thirty active volcanoes in the Philippines. Government warnings in the media instructed all those living within a twelve-mile radius of Pinatubo to evacuate for their own safety and there were regular broadcasts on the US military television network. American scientists were monitoring the volcano's activity and we were assured that Subic, thirty miles to the west of Pinatubo, was a safe area.

The following afternoon I was driving back from Olongapo with Dondie and as we neared Subic we saw that the market place was full of people all gazing upwards and pointing. There was a huge puff of grey smoke coming from the direction of Pinatubo. Like the rest, we were awed rather than frightened by this spectacular but distant phenomenon. Tourists, Dondie had told me, came in large numbers to see the volcano in his home province of Bicol, especially when it was erupting, and it had never caused any danger in his lifetime.

On Friday morning we woke to find the garden of the Servicemen's Home lying under a thin covering of powdery light grey ash, like freshly fallen snow. Carlo and Monique were delighted; the Philippines never see snow, so it was an exciting novelty for them. Later on I had lunch on the base, a farewell party for a friend whose husband was being transferred elsewhere, and in the early evening, before going back to the base for the Friday Bible study, Dondie and I were planning to go house-hunting in Olongapo.

The restrictions on the movements of servicemen were hampering the work of the Home to such an extent that relocation to Olongapo, which unlike Subic was not off limits, seemed the only option. We didn't expect to be living in the new Home for long ourselves, because we'd had news at last that the Pedersons were hoping to return quite soon, but as Lora, the cook, would continue to work there after we'd left we invited her to join us in inspecting the property we had in mind.

We set off in the car in good time, but before we'd gone more than half a mile the sky went suddenly dark, not a rare occurrence in the rainy season. The rain, however, when it began to fall, turned out not to be rain at all, but mud, which spattered heavily onto the windscreen. The windscreen wipers achieved nothing other than to smear the thickly falling mud more effectively all over the surface of the glass, and with visibility down to virtually nil Dondie carefully turned the car in the direction of home. There was a fair amount of traffic and if other drivers hadn't exercised similar caution there could have been serious accidents.

With the help of a container of water begged from a

nearby house, and by stopping every minute or two to wash the mud from the windscreen, we made the half-mile journey home in just less than an hour, to find on arriving that the electricity had been cut off. We had no batteries for the radio so we went to bed that night no wiser as to what was happening and with no information about what it might signify.

Mud was no longer falling when we woke on Saturday, which was my birthday, and instead everything was covered by an inch of dark grey ash. I wasn't immune to the novelty myself this time and getting out my camera I happily finished the film taking shots of the strangely transformed landscape. There was still no electricity, so the radio remained dumb.

We had a busy day ahead. Joseph was to graduate from his Bible school in Angeles City and we planned to take a party of rehab residents and church members to attend the ceremony. Before that, straight after breakfast, I walked with Lora to the local store to buy some noodles, and flour for a cake, as it was something of a tradition for her to bake a cake when anyone had a birthday. It was only 8.30 when we got there, but the store was already packed with frantic shoppers hastily snatching at everything in sight, and the stock of tinned goods especially was disappearing rapidly. These people had obviously heard something we hadn't. Alarmed, we spent what little money we had with us on groceries and candles and I figured I'd have to come back with more money for a second foray.

But while we were still in the store, without warning the sky went dark as if a black curtain had suddenly fallen, instantaneously cutting off the light. Seconds later, ash, mud and stones began to rain down and there was a stampede for the checkout as panic-stricken people rushed to get home and out of danger. Lora and I joined the exodus and were soon liberally plastered with falling mud as we picked our way as quickly as we dared through the murk.

Back at the Home, lit by candles and the gas lamps kept for emergencies, we all sat and waited for the daylight which we felt sure must soon return. But over an hour later we were still marooned in our tiny island of light, with the thick darkness outside pressing blackly against the windows. Mid-morning brought the first of a series of minor earth tremors and at each one I felt a thrill of fear, remembering the devastation caused by a killer quake less than a year ago in Baguio City and Nueva Ecija. In an effort to keep a grip on normality, Lora prepared lunch (the cooker thankfully worked on Calor gas) and even went on to bake my birthday cake. It was a brave attempt, but impossible to sustain as the hours wore on.

It began to thunder, ear-shattering detonations that shook the ground and engulfed us in a solid wave of sound which terrified Carlo and Monique. In the intervals between the thunder cracks we heard the steady bombard-ment of stones bouncing off the corrugated iron roof, and the softer thudding of ash and mud. The ash fall had to be deep by now, but exactly how deep we couldn't tell because the only relief from the blackness outside came from flashes of lightning which shot across the sky like vivid streaks of red fire.

I'd often found comfort in difficult times by setting down my thoughts in a letter, and as the long afternoon drew to a close I sat in the candlelight and wrote to my parents.

Dear Mum and Dad,

How I wish I were back home with you now. Of all my experiences here so far (and I've been through and seen a lot) this is by far the worst – and on my birthday too! The volcano has been blowing all day and the whole area is covered by a black cloud of volcanic ash. It's now 5 o'clock and we haven't had an hour's daylight since early morning. We've been without elec-tricity since yesterday, and earlier today the water supply was cut off too. All day it's been raining volcanic clay, like wet cement, which must be deeper than six inches in the garden.

The thunder and lightning are bad enough to frighten even Dondie, and Monique is so scared we've been singing songs about Jesus to soothe her. Even as I'm writing we keep having minor earthquakes which make us want to get out of the house in case it collapses – except that the ash is so deep and stones are still raining down with the ash and clay.

Almost all the trees in the garden have just crashed down under the weight of the clay. Dondie is worried that the roof will be the next thing to give way, but doing anything about it means going outside, and the lightning is so scary. There's still no sign of light, so who knows how much longer the ash will go on falling?

There goes another earthquake. If it's frightening for us, how much worse must it be for those who don't trust the Lord in situations like this? It makes a big difference being a mother – I know I wouldn't be nearly as anxious if I didn't have the children to think about. I'm terrified to let them out of my sight in case a bigger earthquake comes, but I have to pretend I'm not worried because when Monique is afraid she looks to me for security. Oh Lord, I just wish this whole thing were over. Even if we needed to evacuate the house we couldn't go anywhere; the car is buried in clay, and the ash is too deep to drive through.

Dust is getting into the house now, covering absolutely everything. The only room that's free of it is the main bedroom, but the earthquakes feel so much stronger up there and if a big one came we'd be in trouble if we were upstairs. I don't think I can take much more of this. . . .

It's almost 8 o'clock, and we're still in total darkness. Monique and Carlo are giggling away now without a care in the world. Dondie and I just keep praying. This is the most frightening experience I've ever had. Still no water, and it will be at least another twenty-four hours before the electricity is reconnected, even if the volcano has died down by morning so that the engineers can begin work. . . .

Lora has just come back from her house with her son Christopher. He's thirteen. It's a little after 1am and we've been listening to the radio, using the batteries from Christopher's torch. It seems the earthquakes are a quite separate phenomenon, nothing to do with the volcano. We didn't listen for long because Dondie needed the torch. He's up on the roof now, shovelling off the ash while Christopher holds the torch for him. At least it's only ash falling now, not mud. While it's dry, the ash is much lighter than the mud, but we have to clear it in case there's rain during the night. It must be eighteen inches deep on the ground, even three feet in some places . . .

Monique and Carlo are both asleep. I'm tired too, but I daren't sleep for fear there might be a stronger earthquake. It's 3am and Dondie has just come down off the roof; he hasn't finished yet, but he's completely exhausted. A lot of houses nearby have already fallen under the weight of the mud and we're worried about the balcony over the lounge because it's pretty deep on there too. Poor Lora is trying to clear it . . .

Dondie's back on the roof, worn out but still working. Every time he hears another house cave in it makes him more determined to go on. And we haven't even started on Lora's house yet. We're still having earthquakes, but not so strong, and it's raining now, normal rain that is, so we might see some daylight tomorrow.

Well, my birthday is over and I can honestly say it's been the most memorable I've ever had. I've never been so scared in all my life. I don't know what I'd have done if I hadn't been able to pray.

Can't wait to be home.

Love, Chrissy

After a few hours' sleep we woke on Sunday to daylight at last. As far as the eye could see everything was dark grey, but the uniform blanket of ash couldn't hide the destruction the volcano had hurled down. It had been no respecter of persons and the houses of rich and poor, American and Filipino, had suffered equally. Fallen trees lay everywhere and the streets were strewn with electrical cables and telephone wires. From the balcony, as we continued to work at moving the ash, Dondie and I could see countless streams of bewildered refugees laden with sacks of rice, Calor gas bottles, beds, children and bags. One man was carrying a dead body. The ash was too deep for vehicles, and the evacuees had no choice but to walk.

Before the balcony was cleared, we heard news that

our new church building further down the street was seriously damaged and, fearing that the equipment would be pilfered, Dondie rushed off immediately to investigate, calling over his shoulder, 'I'll finish this when I get back.' I stayed on the balcony, and long before Dondie returned a passing friend called out, 'Chrissy, have you heard the latest news? The volcano is going to blow again and it will be worse than yesterday.'

I panicked. Apart from Tess, an eighteen-year-old who often helped us with baby-sitting, I was alone with the children. It had also started to rain heavily and the water on the balcony was being held by the remaining ash and starting to flood back into the house. Heavy lifting might harm my unborn baby, I might even miscarry, but if I did nothing the house could be damaged, endangering all of us, including Carlo and Monique. 'It's no good, I'll have to do it myself,' I thought, picking up the bucket, and for almost an hour I stuck to the back-breaking work of heaving the ash and water over the balcony wall, praying for the strength to go on and for protection for my baby.

Soon after Dondie returned with news that despite extensive damage to the building almost all our equipment had been spared, we spotted twenty or more of our church members from the *barangay* of Pamatawan.

'Where are you off to?' we asked.

'Manila! There's nothing left of Pamatawan, not a house left standing, and we've heard that the volcano is going to erupt again.'

The impracticability of the plan was a measure of the panic people were feeling: with the children and older people in the party it would take them weeks to walk to Manila, quite apart from the fact that they'd be in grave danger if the volcano were to blow again. They were easily persuaded to change their minds and stay with us for a while, which benefited us as well as them because with the help of the men Dondie was able to finish clearing the roof and balcony.

Suddenly Monique let out a loud scream. She'd fallen and banged her head hard on the corner of the stone steps. For me it was the last straw and I cried with her as I tried to comfort her. When she was calm, I slipped into the bedroom to be alone with the Lord. 'Lord, I can't take any more. Please do something so that we don't have to go through it all again.' I opened my Bible. The cataclysm which had overtaken Subic reminded me of the fate of Sodom and Gomorrah, and turning to Genesis I reread the account of their destruction. Abraham had pleaded with God not to sweep away the righteous with the wicked and God had promised to spare the cities if only ten righteous people were found there. 'Lord,' I prayed, 'there are more than ten righteous people here in Subic. For the sake of your own, please don't destroy it.' I felt my anxieties drain away and knew again his peace which passes understanding.

The arrival of Roy, one of the rehab kids, and then the Del Montes, brought welcome reassurance that everyone there was unhurt, and though the building was badly damaged it was not beyond repair. They were short of food, however, and completely out of rice.

The dreaded second eruption never came – at least, not in Subic. The volcano did indeed blow again, but the wind changed direction and carried the ash further north. We were desperately sorry for the people who lived there, knowing only too well what they must be suffering, but it was impossible not to feel relief that Subic had been spared a repeat of yesterday's disaster, which would surely have razed the whole town to the ground. Once again I slipped into my room, this time to thank the Lord for saving us from total destruction.

Dealing with the aftermath of catastrophe was made easier by reason of simple gratitude at being alive, and the difficulties, though many, were a small price to pay for our deliverance.

Even after the volcano had stopped erupting there was

still danger from sulphur in the ash, and for a time we had to mask our mouths and noses during the daytime to protect our lungs. But the most pressing problem was food, both for ourselves and our Pamatawan evacuees and for the rehab, as our present stock of rice would last only a few days. After spending the whole of Monday morning standing in line at the local store where, in order to prevent disorder and panic buying, the customers at the head of the queue had to wait outside while shop assistants fetched the items they wanted, Dondie and I came away with just a few groceries. The price of rice in Subic had risen by a third which, at the rate we consumed it (a 100lb bag every four days at the rehab alone), was more than we could afford.

We decided to clean up the car and hope it would take us as far as Olongapo. After a bit of a push it spluttered into life and we set off along the main road which the Philippine military had been busy clearing for the past twenty-four hours. All the bars in Subic had collapsed and as we drove past what was left of the funeral parlour we saw piles of corpses lying haphazardly among the rubble. It was clear from the number of fallen electricity poles that we could expect to be without power for some time to come.

We stopped en route to offer a lift to a woman who was hoping to reach Manila with her handicapped daughter, and her evaluation of the disaster highlighted a crucial difference between the western worldview and that of the Philippines.

'God is really angry with us,' she said. 'It's obvious he's telling us to put our lives right.' This woman had no personal relationship with the Lord, but she recognised the existence of a spiritual dimension in the situation.

Had the tragedy taken place in the west, most people would have sought to understand it solely in terms of physical cause and effect, paying heed to the explanations of vulcanologists and seismologists and never thinking about their relationship with God. The western nations

have largely lost their fear of God, but the Filipino people
have a definite God-awareness which I believe he will use
to bring the nation back to himself, working good through
even such a calamity as we had suffered.

An hour's drive brought us eventually to Olongapo,
which had been almost as badly hit as Subic. Churches,
schools, hospitals and shops, if not completely flattened,
were fearfully damaged and, more seriously for our
immediate purpose, all the banks were closed. Until we
could draw money from our account we couldn't replenish
our dwindling store of food, but there was no sign as yet of
any attempt to resume normal business. The only thing we
could do was to bring our need to the Lord who says, 'Be
still, and know that I am God' (Ps 46:10).

He answered our prayers just a couple of days later,
when missionary friends from San Fernando managed to
reach us with food and medical supplies. There was enough
and more to see us through the immediate crisis, so we
were even in a position to help others, church members
and neighbours, who were in need.

Water too was in short supply for a while. The Servicemen's Home was connected to the town's water mains, but
the water company had problems with its generator, which
it could only operate for a few hours each day, and during
the brief period when water was actually flowing the
demand was so heavy that not a drop reached our taps.
However, Dondie discovered that from around 2am there
was a slow but steady flow trickling from the pipe in the
garden and he and I would sit by it for a couple of hours
collecting the water in bowls.

Having collected it, we used some to have a bath which
we had to take right there in the garden; there were so
many people sleeping in the house, and to carry the water
indoors would disturb them. It didn't bother Dondie a bit,
but I found it horribly embarrassing to be standing there in
the open in the middle of the night having my bath fully
clothed. Still, it wasn't the first time I'd had to do it. At

least it was dark, and it was certainly better than no bath at all. We didn't throw the water away when we'd finished. We hoarded every drop that was used for bathing or washing clothes – it was far too precious to waste if we were to maintain the most basic standard of hygiene. Imagine (if you can bear to) the problem we faced with thirty people in one house and no water to flush the toilet.

After a week our household shrank back to its normal size when the evacuees returned to Pamatawan to salvage what they could from the debris and start to rebuild their homes and their lives. But there were some things which had gone for ever. As soon as there was light after the eruption, several ships had evacuated all the military personnel from the base to the island of Cebu, and we never saw any of our American friends again. The US decided to pull out of Subic and in fact military bases all over the Philippines were closed the following year. Without the base, the ministry of the Servicemen's Home naturally ended and from then on the Military Mission concentrated on its Home in Japan.

Our own outreach ministries in the schools and prisons came to a sudden halt. Camp Maquinaya had completely collapsed and the inmates were transferred to other prisons, while the roads and bridges to the jails at Iba and San Fernando were impassable and looked like remaining so for some time to come. San Agustin School was totally destroyed, and all the other schools in the area, including our own kindergarten, had discontinued classes. With so little for me to do, Dondie and I agreed that I should go to England earlier than planned to get the children to safety. He would follow later, in time for the baby's birth, leaving Joseph to oversee the church and the Del Montes to run the rehab in his absence.

Though the school and prison ministries were temporarily suspended, God was powerfully at work in the church, many people having been awakened by the disaster to an awareness of their spiritual need. Our numbers were also swelled by members of two other congregations in the area whose pastors had evacuated, leaving their flocks in Dondie's care. We ourselves had no church building, so our meetings were held in the Servicemen's Home.

It was over a month before I was able to leave, and in the end a misunderstanding with the British Consul meant that Carlo couldn't travel with me and Monique, but would have to join us later with Dondie. When eventually the plane took off (our first flight was cancelled after another minor eruption) I breathed a long sigh of relief as the nightmare unreality of the past six weeks fell away behind me, and I began to look ahead to being reunited with my family and the many opportunities which awaited me to speak about our work.

I accepted engagements right up to the eighth month of my pregnancy and when, on 17th December, I gave birth to Nathanael, Dondie was with me, overjoyed to have his heart's desire, a healthy boy.

20

Philippine Outreach Academy

By the time I arrived back in Subic with the three children in the summer of 1992 (Dondie having returned ahead of us in March) the ravages inflicted by the volcano on the rehab and the church had been repaired, and everything there was back to normal. But Pinatubo hadn't finished yet. Lahar, hot volcanic mud, continued to flow from the mountain, and in the rainy season it was washed down into the valleys and low lying areas, causing huge devastation and killing many people. As near as Castillejos, the next town north of Subic where we had our first rehab, four construction workers died when the lahar hit suddenly in the night. Roads were blocked or destroyed and we were cut off for some time from both the San Fernando and Iba jails.

When Pinatubo erupted in June 1991 we had been on the point of beginning our training in preparation for opening our own ACE elementary school, but I delayed setting a fresh date. I'd lost none of the clarity of my original vision, and Roselyn, on whom as headteacher under my direction as principal so much would depend, was as committed to the idea of the school as I was. I hesitated solely because the director of ACE Philippines was not altogether happy either with the fact that our pupils, the graduates of our kindergarten, would include children of non-Christian parents or that we would not be charging fees. While I weighed the respective merits of going ahead with ACE or of adopting an alternative American curriculum I'd heard of, time was running out and it was only after several long nights of prayer that I received the assurance that it was God's will that we should choose ACE. There was little time for further delay if the school were to open in 1993, but at this crucial point we were once more rocked by a calamity as violent and destructive in personal terms as Pinatubo had been materially.

Romy was a devoted father, if inclined to be somewhat overprotective, especially of his daughters, and it was no secret that he strongly disapproved of Roselyn's fiancé Mike, a trainee civil engineer and member of our church. Though Roselyn, at twenty-seven, was three years beyond the age at which Filipino couples could marry without parental consent, Romy forbade her even to be seen walking alone with Mike. Most of the church members understood Romy's attitude and accepted that this was just the way he was, but there was also a lot of sympathy for Mike who, though he'd not been in the fellowship long, was well liked by the young people and endeared himself to everyone by the love and affection with which he always treated Roselyn.

In the New Year of 1993, however, I noticed a change in Roselyn. She said nothing to me, but she and I were very close and something in her manner led me to conjecture that her feelings for Mike had altered. Then Lourdes told me in confidence that Roselyn was planning to break off the engagement. It appeared that there was a side to Mike that no one outside the family, not even Dondie and I, had suspected. He so resented Romy's disapproval that, instead of showing him the respect required of a Filipino towards an older man and the father of his fiancée, he often treated Romy with contempt and there had been some heated exchanges between them. Roselyn, while conceding that her father might have been a little harsh in his dealings with Mike, could no longer contemplate marriage with a man who had reacted as Mike had done.

One evening a few days after this we held a breaking of bread service in the new house at the bottom of the hill below the rehab which Dondie and I had taken at the urging of our trustees, who felt that we needed separate living quarters for our family. Both Roselyn and Mike were there. The fact that they were sitting apart meant nothing, as they were never allowed to sit together in public, but then I saw that there was no engagement ring on Roselyn's finger. Romy would be glad, I thought, but how was Mike taking it?

Two days later, on Thursday afternoon, I was due to go with a team on one of our regular visits to San Agustin School and as usual I went to pick up the rest of the group in the car. Jane Del Monte was already waiting for me with Edilyn, one of the kindergarten teachers, and Joseph's sister Rose, but Roselyn, who was to teach that day, had just gone off somewhere with Mike and hadn't yet returned. Presumably they had things to discuss about the ending of their relationship, I thought, hoping it wouldn't take too long. But the minutes ticked by and in the end we waited so long for Roselyn that we had to call off the trip to San Agustin.

It was so unlike her that I was deeply uneasy, the more so when, some time later, Romy and Lourdes returned from searching for the couple without success. Most of the young people who heard about Roselyn's mysterious disappearance were unperturbed, taking it for granted that she and Mike had eloped, an expedient which was still quite commonly resorted to in the Philippines by couples unable to obtain parental consent to their marriage; the majority of parents would immediately withdraw their objections once the couple had spent a night together. Roselyn, of course, was old enough to marry without her parents' consent, but to the young people it probably appeared that Romy's disapproval was at the root of her disappearance.

It was an explanation which entirely failed to satisfy me. I knew Roselyn and I knew that her love for the Lord and her commitment to her ministry, as well as her self-respect, would never allow her to act so irresponsibly. My fears for her were intensified when Lourdes discovered that none of Roselyn's clothes were missing: it was obvious that she hadn't planned to go away.

Several days passed and still there was no word from Roselyn. Romy and Lourdes, then Dondie and I, all went to Mike's home in Barretto, near Camp Maquinaya, where his parents confirmed that he too hadn't been seen since Thursday afternoon. They promised to let us know if they learned where he was. Dondie, being more used to the Filipino way of thinking and knowing how much Mike wanted to marry Roselyn, was inclined to accept the elopement theory. He felt my anxiety was excessive and discouraged any further discussion between us, so I had to take my trouble to the Lord.

The following Wednesday we had our weekly overnight prayer meeting in the prayer garden which Dondie had constructed at the side of the disused hospital building. It was really just a roof of native materials for shelter, with some benches and a table, and each Wednesday Dondie and I would gather for prayer with a few other rehab residents from 7pm to 3am. While we prayed, I silently asked the Lord to show me where Mike and Roselyn were, and as I asked I saw a vision of a beach house on stilts. The only place I'd ever seen such a house before was at Baloy Beach in Barretto, between Subic and Olongapo, where I'd visited the Fishers before they took over the Servicemen's Home. It was a long beach with close to 100 houses, but I was sure I'd know the right one if I saw it.

I recognised it without difficulty when I drove to the beach later in the day. It was close to the entrance, which surprised me because I'd expected it to be somewhere more secluded. It took only a few minutes to ascertain that the house was empty, and when my enquiries at nearby cottages failed to elicit any news of the missing pair, I drove right to the end of the beach searching for another house that matched the one in my vision. I found nothing, and returned home puzzled but still convinced that Baloy Beach was connected in some way with Roselyn's disappearance.

However, it was that same day which brought us our first definite news and it came from Lourdes' cousin Jenny, who lived in Manila. Jenny phoned through to Lourdes' sister-in-law (neither we nor the Del Montes had a phone) and left a message saying that Roselyn had visited her in Manila and was now with Mike. Lourdes was given a phone number where she could contact Roselyn in a couple of days' time. The message, which seemed deliberately vague and evasive, did nothing to allay my fears and I was full of questions when I went with Lourdes to return the call. The phone was answered not by Roselyn but by Jenny, who told Lourdes that Mike and Roselyn were to be married in Manila in a fortnight's time, on 3rd February. Jenny didn't divulge the couple's present whereabouts, saying only that Lourdes could see her daughter on the day of the wedding at her cousin's house.

The news came as no surprise to Mike's parents, who had broken their promise to tell us if they heard from him. When Dondie and I went to see them we learned that his mother had even been to see him and Roselyn, and she did her best to assure us that Roselyn had run away so that she'd be free to marry Mike. I frankly didn't believe her; I was convinced that Roselyn was caught up in a web of deception and concealment that was certainly not of her own making.

It so happened that a group of us, including Romy and Lourdes, were due to go to Manila on 3rd February for a three-day seminar on leadership training, and Lourdes, who was beginning to come to terms with the inevitability of her daughter's marriage, arranged to leave the seminar to see Roselyn at Jenny's house and attend the wedding. Romy, however, refused to have any part in it. When Lourdes returned I asked how the ceremony had gone.

'The wedding was already over by the time I arrived. They'd been married by a judge in a courtroom, with dozens of other couples in a mass wedding. Mike's mother was their witness. Anyway, they'll be coming home on Saturday because Mike starts a job on Monday.'

'But how was Roselyn? Was she happy?'

'We were never alone so we had no chance to talk, but I must admit she didn't look very happy.'

'Then why did you leave her?' I asked, my voice rising in exasperation.

'Listen, it's done now,' snapped Lourdes. 'They're married. For Roselyn's sake, accept it.'

Lourdes and I never spoke to each other like this; it was a sign of the strain we were all under.

Early on Saturday morning Roselyn and Mike turned up on our doorstep. Mike was too frightened to face Romy alone and wanted Dondie to go with him. Leaving the two men together, I took Roselyn into another room on the pretext of asking her, as her employer, to explain her absence from the kindergarten. As soon as we were alone she needed no persuasion to talk, her words tumbling over each other in her eagerness to unburden herself.

'Sister Chrissy, I'm so sorry, but it was really not my fault.'

Mike had called for her when she finished work at the kindergarten on that Thursday, two days after she'd broken off the engagement, and asked her to take him to her house so that he could retrieve some things of his which he'd left there. As they walked down the hill from the rehab Roselyn noticed a tricycle (motorcycle taxi with passenger sidecar) waiting at the bottom. Turning to ask Mike about it, she realised that he'd dropped back, and just had time to see him throw a bottle into the long grass before he covered her face with a handkerchief soaked in chloroform. Half-conscious, she was forced into the tricycle, and through the haze of chloroform she dimly heard the driver saying, 'I thought you said the two of you planned this together?'

'Sister Chrissy, believe me, with all the strength I had left I begged the tricycle driver to help me, but he wouldn't.'

The tricycle took them to Baloy Beach and stopped at a house near the entrance where one of Mike's friends, the owner of the house, was waiting for them. When both the friend and the tricycle driver ignored her frantic pleas, Roselyn began to scream. Mike bundled her roughly into the house and beat her in the stomach, warning her to keep quiet.

Mike sent his friend to fetch a drink for Roselyn, whose mouth was very dry from the chloroform, and while he was gone she began screaming again. With the speed of a reflex, Mike lunged at her and pounded her brutally in the stomach until she promised to make no more noise.

I shuddered at the thought of Roselyn, so small and slightly built, at the mercy of a man as big and powerful as Mike.

She was terribly thirsty by the time the friend returned with a glass of fruit juice and gulped it down quickly, realising only when she'd almost finished it that it tasted of some kind of drug.

In her helpless and half-conscious state, Mike raped her.

Under the influence of the drug, she fell asleep. Hours later, in the middle of the night, Mike shook her awake and, weak and disoriented from the shock of abduction and the trauma of the rape, fearful too of being beaten again, she offered no resistance when he told her they were going to Manila. He took her to the house of his aunt and uncle who believed his story that he and Roselyn were eloping and welcomed them into their home.

For the next few days Roselyn was virtually a prisoner. She hadn't a peso in her purse and thus no means of getting back to her family, and Mike threatened to kill her and himself if she tried to escape. She discounted the idea of trying to reach a police station because even if she reported the rape the police wouldn't pay her fare home and she'd be stranded in Manila where Mike might easily track her down. She pinned her hopes on gaining the sympathy of Mike's relatives, but this would depend on speaking to them alone and Mike never left the house.

Before they could be married, however, there were legal formalities to complete and documents to obtain, and eventually Mike had to go out. As soon as he'd left, Roselyn told the full story to his aunt who, not being his blood relation, was initially sympathetic. But when she realised that he could face a life sentence if Roselyn's family pressed charges of rape, she changed tack and joined the rest of the family in trying to persuade Roselyn to consent to the marriage.

Finally, Mike slipped up by agreeing to give Roselyn the money to buy some shampoo. It wasn't much, but it would get her to her mother's cousin Jenny and the next time Mike went out she slipped away and took a jeepney to Jenny's house. Here, at last, was someone who would help her to get away. But her hopes were short-lived. Though she lived in Manila, Jenny's mental attitudes were governed by the deeply engrained taboos of the provinces where, for a woman, sexual experience before marriage was an irretrievable scandal. Whatever the circumstances, if her chastity were in question she had forfeited any chance of finding a husband. For Jenny, the avoiding of such a scandal took precedence over Roselyn's happiness and well being, and she ranged herself with Mike's relatives in urging her to go ahead with the wedding.

It wasn't so very rare for these cultural attitudes to be exploited by unscrupulous men if their offers of marriage were refused. They knew that if they succeeded in seducing a woman she would almost certainly agree to marriage in order to preserve her reputation and escape the shame of being labelled unchaste. Mike was unusual only in the degree of brutality and compulsion he employed. Even Roselyn, who knew in her heart that she herself had done nothing wrong, was made to feel guilty and ashamed by Jenny's arguments.

Her last hope vanished early next morning when Mike appeared at Jenny's house to reclaim her. Having guessed where she'd gone, he had easily traced the address in the telephone directory. By his crying and pleading he convinced Jenny that he genuinely loved Roselyn. Worn down by Jenny's repeated urgings, fearing too that Mike would fulfil his threat to kill her if she refused, and with her self-esteem undermined by irrational guilt, Roselyn allowed herself to be taken back. She had no more strength left to fight.

'There was no way I could get home without his help,' she explained. 'I thought my only hope was to marry him and once we were back in Subic I'd be able to run away and maybe find work with my cousin in Hong Kong.'

'But Roselyn, that wouldn't solve anything. There's no divorce in the Philippines and you'd never be free to marry someone else.'

'I know, but I'm prepared to stay single for the rest of my life.'

'He doesn't have the right to ruin your life like that. He kidnapped you, beat you, raped you and forced you into marriage against your will. Now he'll be expecting you to wash and iron his clothes and cook for him for the rest of his life. That can't be what you want. There has to be another way.'

I didn't know a great deal about Philippine law, but I was certain that it must be possible to end this travesty of a marriage.

'Roselyn, I'm sure you could have your marriage annulled.'

'No, Sister Chrissy,' she said in a defeated voice. 'I'll just stay with him for the time being.'

My heart ached for her. She was not only beautiful but gentle, caring and unselfish, the very last person to deserve the harrowing experience she'd been through, and I couldn't bear the thought of allowing her to suffer the consequences of it for the rest of her life. I couldn't understand why she seemed unwilling to let me help her.

'Roselyn, pray about it and think it over before you make up your mind, but remember, the longer you leave it the harder it will be to get an annulment. Don't say anything to Mike – he'll be working away for a week from Monday and you'll be free of him for a while. Tell me then what you've decided. I'll respect whatever decision you make and if you want to annul your marriage I'll do all I can to help you.'

With a faint gleam of hope in her voice she asked, 'Do you really think there's a possibility?'

'I'm sure of it. You were married under duress.'

'But what about the money? It will be very expensive.' This was the reason for her hesitation; she knew the process would involve a large amount which we couldn't afford.

'That's not a factor, the Lord will provide. What matters is what you want to do. And don't even consider Mike's suicide threats. If he could do what he did to you and call that love, it just shows that the person he loves most is himself. He'll never kill himself. Anyway, what do you want to do next week? Do you want to come back to work?' I thought that the nearer she was to us, the safer she'd be.

'Would you mind if I did? I'd love to, but there's bound to be gossip about me. The parents might object and it could damage our reputation.'

I assured Roselyn that I was in no way ashamed of her and that if others misjudged her, God would vindicate her. With that, we rejoined Mike and Dondie before Mike had time to become suspicious, and the four of us set off to see Romy and Lourdes.

They, of course, knew nothing of what had happened, but I managed to convey to them privately the essence of my conversation with Roselyn, stressing that for the moment we had to remain calm and keep up a pretence of ignorance until she had decided what to do. Deeply shocked, they agreed and played their part magnificently during the brief visit. Lourdes also succeeded in extracting from an unwilling Mike, who could find no excuse for refusing so reasonable a request, his permission for Roselyn to spend one last week with her parents when he went away on Monday. When Roselyn went to collect her things from her old bedroom they secured a few precious moments alone with her, which allowed them to assure her of their love and support. Romy, who she'd feared might be of Jenny's opinion, hugged her and promised to move mountains if necessary to free her from the man who called himself her husband.

I shared their anguish as we watched Roselyn walk through the door with Mike. It would be a long weekend.

It took courage for Roselyn to return to work on Monday, knowing that the children's parents suspected that she had eloped. Setting aside her embarrassment she broached the subject herself and told them all frankly that she would never have considered eloping and had left under duress. One mother revealed that she had actually seen Roselyn being taken away in the tricycle and had assumed from her appearance that she was ill and on the way to hospital with Mike. There was no need to disclose any details of her ordeal; all the parents knew and respected her, and contrary to her fears they readily believed that she was not to blame. After her openness with the parents it was no great surprise when, once we were alone, she told me that she wanted to go ahead with the annulment.

'You're quite sure?' I asked.

'Sister Chrissy, I'm so scared of him and what he might do to me that I even have a knife here in my handbag. If I didn't annul the marriage, I'd have to run away.'

That same day I went with the Del Montes to Olongapo

to set in motion the legal process which would set Roselyn free. Ten years' experience of helping so many inmates through their own cases had given me a fairly wide circle of acquaintances among the lawyers and judges, one of whom put me in touch with a sympathetic man who was prepared to represent Roselyn for 15,000 pesos rather than the usual minimum fee of 25,000. I was assured that we had a strong case, especially if Mike could be persuaded not to contest it.

Back in Subic, Colonel Custodio, the chief of police and a kindly man, immediately arranged for Roselyn to make a statement at the police station and have a medical examination. He even went on to speak to several people in our *barangay*, asking them to look out for her safety. At the end of the day I was amazed by how much we'd accomplished and marvelled again at the answer to that prophetic prayer of David Chaudhary's all those years ago. God had indeed given us favour with the authorities.

As a further precautionary measure I arranged for Roselyn to stay with a missionary couple, the Vroomans. I hadn't known them well before Roselyn was abducted, but when I went to them for help they gave it unstintingly, opening their home to her for as long as she needed it. They gave her much more than a place to stay, spending hours talking through with her the irrational feelings of guilt and unworthiness which rape victims so often suffer, until she felt thoroughly assured that she was entirely innocent and had no need to be ashamed.

Before the week ended, news filtered through to Mike who immediately hurried back to Subic to see Dondie and me. He admitted the truth of everything Roselyn had said, but insisted that he loved her and had only wanted to hasten their marriage. He had already repented of his actions, he claimed, but made no demur when Dondie told him firmly that he must find another church. He had not, however, given up hope that Roselyn would return to him and was convinced that the annulment was all Romy's doing.

'Wake up, Mike,' I said. 'Even if she loved you once, how can she love you now after what you've done? She's simply afraid of you. Just be thankful that you're not facing a rape charge. It's over, Mike. Accept it.'

The case came up at the end of March and Roselyn and I were the only ones to give evidence. Mike had taken our advice and did nothing to contest it. I didn't know the judge who presided, but he seemed to be a compassionate man, and as far as I could tell the case appeared to be going well. It was a comfort too to know that in England friends and supporters, who were already hard at work raising the money to cover our legal costs, would be praying for us constantly.

Mercifully, the judge's decision was not long in coming and a few weeks after the conclusion of the case Roselyn received the documents which confirmed that her marriage was annulled and she was free. The mental scars would take longer to heal, but with God's help she could begin to put the past behind her. Our priority now was to do everything to ensure her complete recovery and though it was disappointing to have to postpone the opening of the school yet again, I accepted that it would have to wait until next year. I said nothing of this to Roselyn as she had more than enough to deal with, but it was she herself who raised the subject.

'Sister Chrissy, are we going ahead with the ACE training? We'll be too late if we don't apply soon.'

'But are you sure you're ready for that?'

'Actually, the more I have to do the better I am. It helps to keep my mind occupied and stops me dwelling on what happened to me. I'd much rather be busy.'

Roselyn's courage meant that there remained only one obstacle to the realisation of our long-treasured hopes – the ever present problem of finance. In addition to the teachers' salaries, which would be the biggest item in the budget, we would have to pay ACE eighteen pesos per student each month, plus the cost of the learning materials. There would also have to be a 'learning centre' which would take up most of the remaining space in the rehab, where each student could have an individual 'office' as specified by ACE. These consist of long tables divided by boards into separate cubicles, three offices to a table, the whole structure being easy to disassemble if more space is needed in the learning centre for joint activities.

One day, I was sure, there would be enough sponsors to finance the children through school, but at the moment our resources fell well short. Yet again we brought our problem to the Lord and one night in the prayer garden he spoke to me and assured me that he would meet our need. So it was with confidence that I told Roselyn to make the arrangements for our training. We had no difficulty in finding teachers. In Roselyn we already had the one fully qualified teacher required by the ACE programme and in the appointment of others we had the joy of gathering in the fruit of our past ministry.

Marivic and Lorna had expressed a desire to work for the Lord after graduating from San Agustin School, where I had taught them Scripture in their elementary and high school years, while Edilyn, now nineteen, was one of the firstfruits of our children's outreaches in Pamatawan almost ten years ago and was already teaching in the kindergarten. All three would teach in the mornings and use the money they earned to pay for their training in education at night school, as Roselyn had done. Tina was not a Christian when she enrolled her daughter in our kindergarten. She was converted at one of the meetings we held for parents, was subsequently baptised in the Holy Spirit and became a member of our church. A college graduate, she already had considerable experience of teaching in a private school, though not a Christian one.

Then there was Tess, the eldest child of a poor family,

whom we'd financed through high school in return for help in caring for Monique while I was working in the prisons and children's outreaches. She too intended to use her salary to study education at college. And it was a particular joy to have Dondie's niece Letty join us to help care for the rehab children and teach in the kindergarten. I had a great admiration for Letty who, without help from anyone, had pioneered a small house fellowship in a remote part of her home province of Bicol, where the activities of the NPA made the preaching of the gospel a hazardous undertaking. All of our teachers felt called of God to work at the Philippine Outreach Academy and were willing to do so for whatever salary we were able to pay them.

After we'd taken a step of faith in setting the date for our training, the Lord opened his hand liberally and help of all kinds began to flow in. First of all, the mail brought us a large and totally unexpected money order. Then an ACE school at a church in Lancashire, whose pastor was a friend of Dad's, agreed to send us their used paces, the modules of learning material, like brightly coloured comics, on which the curriculum is based. In the west, pupils write their answers directly onto the pace, but schools in third-world countries such as the Philippines are allowed to blank out the answers in used paces and the children write in notebooks instead.

We also discovered hidden treasure in our new driver, Tony, who joined us when Bill Del Monte returned to his home town in the province of Laguna. Tony, in addition to his skill as a car mechanic, turned out to have a gift for carpentry and he worked long into the night constructing fifteen 'offices' for our first intake of elementary pupils. Fifteen was the number of children graduating from kindergarten that year and it was only to these that the elementary school would be open; our older children who were already following the ACE programme at White Stone Academy would stay there for the sake of continuity.

All was in readiness by the beginning of June and as

enrolment week approached I surveyed the empty school-rooms which would soon be full of eager, happy children. With the addition of the elementary school, the Philippine Outreach Academy was an accomplished reality and by the grace of God would offer to the children of Subic the hope of a better future, both now and in eternity. Neither the fury of Pinatubo nor the personal tragedy which had over-taken Roselyn had been able to prevent the fulfilment of the vision.

It was a time for looking forward, but the future which lay ahead of me was founded on the experiences of the past. In the ten years since God called me to the Philippines he had gone before me, providing for my every need, redeeming my failures and lifting me over obstacles I could never have surmounted myself. Trust him, offer him your nothing, and he can do everything. To him be all the glory.

Afterword

Since the events described in this book, the Lord has given us many fresh challenges and opportunities. The Philippine Outreach Christian Fellowship currently has over ninety adult members (though numbers fall slightly in the rainy season) and has moved to larger premises. When we took it over in December 1994, the building, which had formerly been used as an arena for cockfighting, consisted of just a very rusty roof supported by wooden posts, with seating for a few hundred people; there were no walls and no cement floor. Since then, as we did with the rehab, we have been renovating it as and when we can.

Dondie and I both feel that the Lord is now leading us to extend the work beyond Subic and to plant four or five churches in other provinces of the Philippines. We have also been praying for revival, asking the Lord for 5,000 souls by the year 2000. Our vision for the future is shared by Joseph who, having pioneered a church in another *barangay* of Subic after graduating from Bible school, has returned to us as assistant pastor.

Two of the Christian inmates in San Fernando Jail are praying that on their release they might be involved with us in planting a church in the town of San Fernando. While still in the jail, they are leading Bible studies in their cells and one of them has been acting as my interpreter while Romy and Lourdes take a training course with YWAM. At Iba Jail, where we have been able to start the Iba Christian Inmates' Fellowship, the inmates have their own meeting room which, by means of their tithes and offerings and gifts from visitors, they have furnished and decorated themselves. Our ministry at Camp Maquinaya came to an end when Pinatubo erupted and so far we have been unable to resume it, but recently the way ahead has become clear and we shall be looking to the Lord to show us the right time to begin visiting there again.

The Philippine Outreach Academy has grown too, with the addition of a high school section to the pre-school, kindergarten and elementary levels, and all of our graduates have passed the national college entrance exam. Two of them have received scholarships to pay for their college courses and another, a talented musician who wants to use his gift to serve the Lord, has gained a place at music college in Manila; we are praying that funds will become available to finance him on the course. Three other graduates will be working part time at the Philippine Outreach Academy to support themselves through college.

Since we first started the Academy, government schools have greatly improved, though class sizes are still large (often more than sixty pupils) and ACE students continue to perform better than those from government schools. The general standard of living in the Philippines is rising too, but the very poor tend to get left behind and it is still our aim to offer them the lifeline of education as a way of escape from their poverty.

Our son Carlo is thirteen, and a Philippine Outreach high school student; as well as playing the drums in church services, he plays the guitar and is having piano lessons. His sister Monique, now eight, has reached grade three in our elementary school and is also learning to play the piano, while Nathanael, at five, has just started grade one. He wants to play the drums like his *kuya* (older brother). We have two more sons now: three-year-old Rannel, who has recently enrolled in our nursery, and Aaron, who will soon be two.

Since the school takes up ninety per cent of the rehab building we have no spare accommodation and cannot take in more ex-prisoners at present. But this is, I believe, only a temporary state of affairs. The old hospital next to the rehab still lies empty, waiting for us to enter into the promise of the Lord. 'For the vision is yet for an appointed time. . . . Though it tarries, wait for it; Because it will surely come. . .' (Hab 2:3).

Only Love Can Make A Miracle

Mahesh Chavda with John Blattner

*'Suddenly I became aware of a brilliant white light...
I turned and saw a man walking towards me. I knew
immediately who it was. It was Jesus.'*

Mahesh Chavda grew up in Mombasa, Kenya, the son
of a prominent Hindu teacher. He grew disillusioned
and turned to the Bible. One night God spoke to him in
a powerful vision, and he gave his life to Christ.

As a graduate student in Texas, he was gripped by the
power of the Spirit. Almost despite himself an
extraordinary ministry developed: travelling
worldwide he would be used by God to cast out evil
spirits, raise the dead, give sight to the blind and lead
thousands and thousands to Christ. This ministry
among the world's poor continues today.

'This book is a must!' – TERRY VIRGO

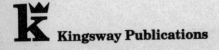

Kingsway Publications

The Long Way Home

Gordon Barley with Mike Fearon

Gordon Barley was a man for whom the phrase *'sex and drugs and rock 'n' roll'* might have been invented.

Gordon longed to see the world, to experience everything that was on offer to those who were young in the seventies and eighties. His appetite for life seemed insatiable. Yet long-term relationships frightened him. Emotional highs deserted him. Even religion missed the mark.

At the end of his wanderings Gordon found himself back in his native East End of London, faced once again with the challenges of his youth. Had he come so far, only to find the answers he sought on his own doorstep?

'This is an honest, upfront account of a modern man's search for truth. It is the story of a physical and spiritual journey through countries and creeds. A fascinating read!'

– JILL DANDO

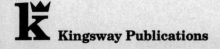

Kingsway Publications

Classic Real Life Stories

The complete and unabridged text of three Kingsway testimony books:

- *Vanya* by Myrna Grant – the story of a Russian soldier who was also a Christian during the worst excesses of religious persecution.

- *Blood Brothers* by Elias Chacour with David Hazard – the story of Elias Chacour's search for peace in his homeland of Palestine.

- *Streetwise* by John Goodfellow with Andy Butcher – the testimony of a one-time streetfighter and criminal who became a Christian and went back to the streets with hope for others.

Three books in one – great value and a great read!

K Kingsway Publications